Quality-Assurance Plan for Groundwater Activities, U.S. Geological Survey, Washington Water Science Center

By Mark D. Kozar and Sue C. Kahle

Open-File Report 2013-1151

U.S. Department of the Interior
U.S. Geological Survey

U.S. Department of the Interior
SALLY JEWELL, Secretary

U.S. Geological Survey
Suzette M. Kimball, Acting Director

U.S. Geological Survey, Reston, Virginia: 2013

For more information on the USGS—the Federal source for science about the Earth,
its natural and living resources, natural hazards, and the environment,
visit http://www.usgs.gov or call 1–888–ASK–USGS.

For an overview of USGS information products, including maps, imagery, and publications,
visit http://www.usgs.gov/pubprod

To order this and other USGS information products, visit http://store.usgs.gov

Suggested citation:
Kozar, M.D., and Kahle, S.C., 2013, Quality-assurance plan for groundwater activities, U.S. Geological Survey,
Washington Water Science Center: U.S. Geological Survey Open-File Report 2013-1151, 88 p.,
http://pubs.usgs.gov/ofr/2013/1151/.

Contents

Conversion Factors and Datums

Conversion Factors

Inch/Pound to SI

Multiply	By	To obtain
Length		
inch (in.)	2.54	centimeter (cm)
inch (in.)	25.4	millimeter (mm)
foot (ft)	0.3048	meter (m)
Volume		
pint (pt)	0.4732	liter (L)
quart (qt)	0.9464	liter (L)
gallon (gal)	3.785	liter (L)
gallon (gal)	0.003785	cubic meter (m^3)
gallon (gal)	3.785	cubic decimeter (dm^3)

SI to Inch/Pound

Multiply	By	To obtain
Length		
centimeter (cm)	0.3937	inch (in.)
millimeter (mm)	0.03937	inch (in.)
meter (m)	3.281	foot (ft)
Volume		
liter (L)	0.2642	gallon (gal)
cubic meter (m^3)	264.2	gallon (gal)
cubic decimeter (dm^3)	0.2642	gallon (gal)

Datums

Vertical coordinate information is referenced to the North American Vertical Datum of 1988 (NAVD 88).

Horizontal coordinate information is referenced to the North American Datum of 1983 (NAD 83).

Altitude, as used in this report, refers to distance above the vertical datum.

Quality-Assurance Plan for Groundwater Activities, U.S. Geological Survey, Washington Water Science Center

by Mark D. Kozar and Sue C. Kahle

Abstract

This report documents the standard procedures, policies, and field methods used by the U.S. Geological Survey's (USGS) Washington Water Science Center staff for activities related to the collection, processing, analysis, storage, and publication of groundwater data. This groundwater quality-assurance plan changes through time to accommodate new methods and requirements developed by the Washington Water Science Center and the USGS Office of Groundwater. The plan is based largely on requirements and guidelines provided by the USGS Office of Groundwater, or the USGS Water Mission Area. Regular updates to this plan represent an integral part of the quality-assurance process. Because numerous policy memoranda have been issued by the Office of Groundwater since the previous groundwater quality assurance plan was written, this report is a substantial revision of the previous report, supplants it, and contains significant additional policies not covered in the previous report.

This updated plan includes information related to the organization and responsibilities of USGS Washington Water Science Center staff, training, safety, project proposal development, project review procedures, data collection activities, data processing activities, report review procedures, and archiving of field data and interpretative information pertaining to groundwater flow models, borehole aquifer tests, and aquifer tests. Important updates from the previous groundwater quality assurance plan include: (1) procedures for documenting and archiving of groundwater flow models; (2) revisions to procedures and policies for the creation of sites in the Groundwater Site Inventory database; (3) adoption of new water-level forms to be used within the USGS Washington Water Science Center; (4) procedures for future creation of borehole geophysics, surface geophysics, and aquifer-test archives; and (5) use of the USGS Multi Optional Network Key Entry System software for entry of routine water-level data collected as part of long-term water-level monitoring networks.

Introduction

The Water Mission Area (WMA; previously organized as the Water Resources Discipline, or WRD) of the U.S. Geological Survey (USGS) performs a wide variety of groundwater data-collection programs and investigations to assess the status of the Nation's groundwater resources. Results of these activities are used to aid the Nation in characterizing, developing, managing, and maintaining its groundwater resources. As the Nation's principal earth-science agency, the USGS collects accurate data and produces factual and impartial interpretive reports. Methods for data collection and analysis developed by the USGS have become standard techniques used by numerous federal, state, and local agencies, and by private enterprises. Additionally, data collected by scientific organizations such as the USGS are being used increasingly by the public to define and examine various natural-resource and environmental problems. As a result, scientific organizations are being challenged to demonstrate the credibility of their data on the basis of objective evidence rather than on the organization's history and reputation.

To address these demands and expectations, the USGS implemented a program in 1997 that is designed to ensure that all scientific work done by, or for, the USGS, is conducted in accordance with a quality-assurance (QA) program. The Office of Ground Water (OGW) within the WMA has the responsibility of developing, coordinating, and implementing the quality-assurance program for Water Science Center groundwater activities. As part of that program, the OGW prepared a Groundwater Quality-Assurance Plan (Burnett and others, 1997) that covers all groundwater activities by USGS Water Science Centers. Additionally, USGS reports (Schroder and Shampine, 1992) and (Shampine and others, 1992) outline the general guidelines for preparing Science Center QA plans, and for integrating QA into project work plans. Guidelines presented here are intended to supplement these three reports and update the previous Washington Water Science Center QA plan (Drost, 2005) to provide specific details related to groundwater activities within the USGS Washington Water Science Center (WAWSC).

A QA plan can be defined as a formal document that describes the management policies, objectives, principles, organizational authority, responsibilities, accountability, and implementation of a responsible organizational unit or group for ensuring quality in its products. The implementation of a groundwater data QA plan will enhance groundwater data collected by the USGS personnel of the WAWSC by providing for the following:

1. Consistency (across projects, science centers, mission areas, and so forth)
2. Accountability (to client, scientific community, and regulatory agencies)
3. Comparability (yields results of known quality)
4. Traceability (written record of how, who, and when work was performed, training, equipment, and so forth)
5. Repeatability (documentation of technique that leads to the comparable results time after time with the same accuracy)

This groundwater quality-assurance plan (GWQAP) provides formal procedures for documentation and review of policies, practices, and activities that are used by USGS, WAWSC, to assure the technical quality and reliability of WAWSC groundwater products. The plan is based on the following principles:

- WAWSC groundwater programs and projects will be planned to efficiently and effectively provide information needed to evaluate local, state, and national water resources.

- Technical and scientific activities will be performed in accordance with applicable USGS Water Mission Area and OGW practices and policies.

- Groundwater activities will be performed by technically qualified personnel performing at a level commensurate with their training and experience.

- All such activities and projects will receive appropriate and timely review for completeness, reliability, and scientific merit.

- Remedial actions will be taken to correct any observed technical or project deficiency.

- Safety procedures, training, and equipment will be provided to minimize hazards and protect field personnel.

Organization and Responsibilities

The responsibilities for conducting, organizing, and reviewing Water Science Center groundwater projects, data collection, and other activities are outlined in the GWQAP (Brunett and others, 1997) available at *http://water.usgs.gov/ogw/pubs/OFR9711/index.html*. Although QA is a personal responsibility of all employees of the USGS, ultimate QA responsibility within each science center lies with the Center Director. Clear statements of specific responsibilities promote an understanding of the role of each employee in the overall process of assuring quality, and can help to prevent errors and deficiencies that may otherwise occur. Implementation and follow-up responsibilities lie with data-collection staff, project chiefs, section chiefs, discipline specialists, center directors, regional specialists, and others. Even if QA responsibilities are ancillary duties for some employees, these functions are documented in this report.

The following USGS WAWSC personnel are responsible for carrying out the provisions of the GWQAP:

1. Center Director
2. Center Groundwater Specialist
3. Associate Director for Hydrologic Studies and Assistant Director for Hydrologic Data
4. Studies Program Section Chiefs
5. Data Program Field Office Chiefs
4. Center Groundwater Database Administrators
5. Center Groundwater Project Chiefs
6. Other WAWSC scientists and technicians, as needed for selected groundwater activities, particularly synoptic well sampling, water-level measurements, or base-flow stream seepage surveys

Center Director

The Center Director is responsible for:

1. Managing and directing the WAWSC program, including all groundwater activities
2. Ensuring that groundwater activities in the center meet the needs of cooperating agencies, including state and local agencies, the general public, and the Federal Government
3. Ensuring that all aspects of this GWQAP are understood and followed by center personnel
4. Providing final resolution of any conflicts or disputes related to groundwater activities within the center
5. Ensuring that technical reviews of all groundwater activities are conducted
6. Ensuring that all publications and other technical communications released by the center are accurate and in accordance with USGS policy

Groundwater Specialist

The Center Groundwater Specialist duties include, but are not limited to:

1. Working with the Center Director and Section Chiefs to maintain current groundwater technical expertise for the center
2. Maintaining the groundwater technical-procedure documents file
3. Consulting with the center staff on groundwater technical matters and keeping center personnel briefed on procedural and technical communications from Region and Headquarters
4. In consultation with Section Chiefs, advising on training needs for personnel engaged in groundwater activities
5. Participating in technical reviews of groundwater activities
6. Reviewing groundwater related project proposals
7. Reviewing groundwater related project reports
8. Overseeing calibration checks on tapes, pressure transducers, and other equipment.
9. In consultation with the Section Chiefs, providing project chiefs with technical and administrative support as needed

Section Chiefs and Associate and Assistant Directors

The Associate and Assistant Directors, Studies Program Section Chiefs, and Data Program Field Office Chiefs are responsible for:
1. Managing and directing groundwater activities assigned to their section, and ensuring that the stated objectives are met in a timely manner
2. Reviewing work plans for groundwater programs and projects
3. In consultation with the Center Groundwater Specialist, providing project chiefs with technical and administrative support as needed
4. Creating (with personnel in the section) a training plan for each employee, where appropriate
5. Reviewing groundwater reports under their direction
6. Monitoring progress of groundwater project chiefs in implementing this plan for their respective projects
7. Alerting the Center Groundwater Specialist or Senior Management Team of potential problems related to groundwater activities under their direct supervision
8. Ensuring (in consultation with the Center Groundwater Specialist) that groundwater training is incorporated into each person's training plan, where appropriate.

Groundwater Database Administrator

The primary Center Groundwater Database Administrator (GWSI DBA) is responsible for:
1. In consultation with Project Chiefs and the Center Groundwater Specialist, assuring that all site inventories and water-level data are entered into the Groundwater Site Inventory (GWSI) Database in a timely and accurate manner
2. In cooperation with the Center Groundwater Specialist, assuring that all project staff are properly trained in the process of well inventory and in the collection of water-level data. This will include working with field office personnel to assure they are trained in the proper use of the Multi

Optional Network Key Entry System (MONKES) software for storage and update of water-level data collected in the field

3. Notifying the Center Groundwater Specialist and appropriate Project Chiefs of any site inventory coding sheets or water-level measurements provided by project staff that are not consistent with USGS WAWSC or USGS policy.

4. In cooperation with the Center Groundwater Specialist, assisting in the quality assurance/quality control (QA/QC) of steel tapes, electrical tapes, and other routine groundwater equipment used for well inventory and water-level measurements in the field

Project Chiefs

The groundwater Project Chiefs are responsible for:

1. Directing and conducting the technical work of the project, including all phases of data collection, data review, data storage, data analysis, and report preparation, according to appropriate procedures

2. Communicating project plans, progress, and problems to supervisors by providing written progress reports at periodic reviews

3. Preparing written work plans, documenting project activities, and ensuring that data are placed in the USGS National Water Information System (NWIS) data base, as appropriate, prior to project termination

4. In consultation with the GWSI DBA and the Center Groundwater Specialist, assuring that all site inventories and water-level data are entered into the Groundwater Site Inventory (GWSI) Database in a timely and accurate manner

5. In consultation with the GWSI DBA and the Center Groundwater Specialist, advising of upcoming field efforts, including well inventories, synoptic or monthly water-level runs, and baseflow surveys, to assure that sufficient resources and funds are allocated for site creation and water-level data entry tasks

6. Maintaining a project file containing memoranda, oral or written communications, technical-procedure documents used, original data, and other documentation

7. Ensuring that project activities are carried out in a timely manner.

8. Creating, with the supervisor, a personal training plan

9. Archiving project files, at the completion of the project

10. Archiving groundwater-flow or solute-transport models, borehole- or surface-geophysics data, or aquifer-test data collected for the project. Groundwater flow models and aquifer tests must be submitted through the Center Groundwater Specialist to the Regional Groundwater Specialist for approval prior to archival

Scientists and Technicians

Other scientists and technicians collecting or processing groundwater data within the WAWSC are responsible for:

1. Familiarizing themselves with the protocols and requirements of the GWQAP, and assuring that

field collection of data, transmission of water-levels, GWSI site inventory coding sheets, aquifer test data, and other data meet specifications called for in the GWQAP

2. Communicating with Project Chiefs, the Center Groundwater Specialist, and the GWSI DBA, as appropriate, any problems with field collection of data or deviations from the protocols established within the GWQAP

3. Ensuring that field data are transmitted to the GWSI or QWDATA DBAs in a timely and accurate manner

Training and Safety

The qualifications of project personnel relative to the technical demands of the work will be determined by the Project Chief, Section Chiefs, and discipline specialists; training to remedy deficiencies will be recommended. Personnel will receive training to ensure technical competence. The appropriate Section or Field Office Chief will develop and document a specific plan to provide the required training. The WAWSC will perform all QA activities related to training, as documented in Brunett and others (1997, p. 7). The Center Groundwater Specialist will disseminate notices of upcoming USGS National Training Center (NTC), regional training courses, WEBEX seminars, or other pertinent training to Section Chiefs and WAWSC groundwater staff, and solicit input from the various Section Chiefs on groundwater training needs of staff in their sections. The Center Groundwater Specialist, in consultation with the Section and Field Office Chiefs, will also recommend specific training when needed.

The safety of personnel is a priority for the USGS and the WAWSC. The WAWSC communicates information and directives related to safety to all personnel through in-house and out-of-office training classes, memoranda, and internet web seminars, to assure that personnel follow established safety procedures and policies.

In the WAWSC, the designated Safety Officer heads the WAWSC Safety Committee, identifies and provides direction on safety issues, manages the safety budget, coordinates safety training, prepares safety reports for the Regional Office, and deals with new and ongoing safety issues. Currently, the Water Mission Area provides policy and guidelines for safety-related issues in the WAWSC. The Safety Committee, which meets periodically, consists of nine members: the WAWSC Safety Officer, the WAWSC Center Director, one member from each of the three Field Offices, one member representing administration and management, and one specialist each in aviation, hazardous waste, and boat safety.

Job Hazard Analyses (JHAs) list the basic tasks of projects, identify the potential hazards associated with the anticipated tasks, and help develop safety procedures to avoid the hazards. JHAs are required for all projects, and it is the responsibility of the project chief to assure that required JHAs are developed for groundwater-related activities, including, but not limited to, well inventories, measuring water levels, measuring stream base flow as part of seepage surveys, conducting aquifer tests, and collecting borehole geophysics data. For long-term water-level monitoring at individual wells, site specific JHAs are required, particularly for real-time wells or sites with site specific hazards. Blanket JHAs are applicable for new sites where specific hazards are not known. WAWSC personnel who have questions or concerns pertaining to safety, or who have suggestions for improving some aspect of safety, should direct those questions, concerns, and suggestions to their supervisor, or the Center Safety Officer.

Individuals working on hazardous waste sites are subject to strict guidelines, which require a minimum of 40 initial hours of OSHA hazardous waste operations and response (HAZWOPER) certification, and annual 8-hour refresher training. Additionally, medical monitoring may be required and certification for use and annual fit test of air purifying respirators (APRs) and self-contained breathing apparatus (SCBA) may also be required. Due to the site specific nature of hazardous waste studies, WAWSC personnel working on hazardous waste sites must coordinate with the WAWSC Safety Officer to assure that all legal, medical, and site specific requirements are strictly adhered to.

Project Planning and Reviews

Project planning includes staffing and preparation of a detailed project work plan and budget. The various Section Chiefs, along with the Associate Director for Hydrologic Studies, are responsible for the selection of project chiefs (team leaders), but the selection will be made in consultation with the WAWSC Center Director, Discipline Specialists, and other Section Chiefs, as appropriate. Projects will receive technical and budget reviews on a periodic schedule as determined by the Associate Director for Hydrologic Studies, in consultation with the Center Discipline Specialists and individual Project Chiefs.

Development of Project Proposals and Work Plans

WAWSC policy provides specific guidelines for the development of proposals and work plans for new projects. Much of the policy is based on existing and proposed guidelines provided by the USGS. The most recent guidance from the USGS Water Mission Area (WMA policy memorandum 2013.01) provides detailed guidance for the development of project proposals. Discussions of mandatory elements for project proposals and work plans are provided within this GWQAP to guide WAWSC personnel in preparation and transmittal of project proposals and work plans.

Project Proposals

The development of a project proposal and work plan typically begins in discussions, either with a cooperator or amongst WAWSC personnel, regarding a groundwater problem or information need. At this point, the project chief, in consultation with the appropriate WAWSC Discipline Specialists, Section Chiefs, and experienced groundwater personnel, develops a project proposal. Generally, the proposal will indicate the overall purpose, scope, objectives, strategy, duration, general personnel requirements, funding, and expected products of the study. The WAWSC has detailed instructions on the development of project proposals, as part of the Project Development Toolbox that is accessible to Center staff via the WAWSC intranet site. In addition, Water Mission Area Memorandum No. 13.01 establishes policies and provides specific requirements for the mandatory elements that must be included in any proposal sent to the Water Science Field Team (WSFT) for approval. WAWSC personnel are referred to this memo (appendix 2) for guidance on development and submission of proposals.

WAWSC policy requires significant review of potential project proposals. The purpose of the review is: (1) to assure that tasks outlined in the proposal are consistent with USGS and WAWSC policy, (2) to assure the approach is reasonable and can successfully meet study objectives, and (3) to assure that appropriate personnel, time, and funds are available to meet study goals and deliverables. Proposals must specify all data needs, work elements, technical approaches, itemized costs, personnel needs, and a timeline for completion of specific work elements. Any components of the study that will be completed by cooperators or by contractors also should be clearly documented. Cost estimates for each of the project tasks should be estimated from current budget spreadsheets obtained from the WAWSC Budget Analyst or Administrative Officer.

Internal review of proposals will include, at a minimum, review by the appropriate Section Chief and the Center Groundwater Specialist. If the project is multi-disciplinary, review by Center Water-Quality or Surface-Water Specialists may be required. Additional review by the Center Safety Officer to address potential safety issues related to the project and by the Administrative Officer with respect to financial aspects of potential joint funding agreements (JFAs) is also required. Finally, if wells or sites will be inventoried or if water-level data will be collected for the project, the GWSI DBA also must be consulted, and sufficient resources budgeted to assure that project data are entered into GWSI. Upon completion of the internal review process, the proposal will be submitted to the Water Science Field Team (WSFT) Chief, who will route the proposal to the appropriate Discipline Specialists. The WSFT then recommends approval of the proposal to the Northwest Regional Director. Upon approval by the Northwest Regional Director, the proposal will be developed into a detailed work plan. This generally involves a literature search of applicable reports, and some limited field reconnaissance. The work plan summarizes data needs and technical approaches, identifies work elements, itemizes costs, defines personnel needs, and provides deadlines for each work element. Requirements for work by the Science Publishing Network and the Information Technology Section, by the cooperator, or by contractors will be clearly identified and scheduled. Coordination with the WAWSC Outreach Coordinator is also required as part of WAWSC policy to produce internet web pages for each project.

Project Work Plans

A report-planning document may be developed as an integral part of the project work plan. The planning document will identify the type, scope, intended audience, and planned reports, and will provide a preliminary outline of each report, including a description of major illustrations and tables. Preparation of the work plan and report-planning documents is to be accomplished in the first 10 percent of the project duration. To achieve this end, the project leader confers with the appropriate Section Chief, the WAWSC Groundwater Specialist, and any other persons, USGS or non-USGS, who may offer guidance or insight into the problem being investigated.

The work plan and report-planning document will meet the financial and temporal limits already placed on the study in the approved project proposal, and will schedule the submission of the final report(s) so that the report(s) will be published prior to the conclusion of project funding. The work plan will include a completed Report Processing Schedule. The work plan will be reviewed by the Associate Director for Hydrologic Studies, the appropriate Section Chief, other Discipline Specialists as appropriate, Reports Specialist, and the WAWSC Center Director. Review also may be sought from Regional or Headquarters personnel, or from the cooperating agency. The project chief will develop a final work plan and report plan in response to the review comments.

If, during development of the work plan (or at any other time during the life of the project), it becomes clear that the technology, funding, personnel, or time indicated in the original project proposal are inadequate to meet project objectives, the Project Chief will inform the Associate Director for Hydrologic Studies, who may then direct the Project Chief to complete two modified versions of the work plan. In one of these versions, the objectives will be reduced to fit the originally-estimated resources; in the other version, the resources will be increased to meet the original objectives. These two plans, after appropriate internal review, will form the basis for further negotiations between the cooperating agency and the WAWSC staff on modifications to the originally approved proposal. A final plan will be developed from the results of these negotiations. If at any time the scope of the project must be modified from the scope described in the approved proposal and work plan, these modifications must be agreed upon by the WAWSC and the cooperating agency, and must be documented by the Project Chief.

The general project personnel requirements will be determined during the proposal process. Personnel assignments become more specific as the work plan is developed. As the need for each employee position on the project is established, selection procedures will be initiated and the personnel assembled. This process will normally overlap the process of developing the work plan.

Project Review

All groundwater projects will receive technical review by the Groundwater Specialist and the Associate Director for Hydrologic Studies at approximately 4-month intervals during the life of the project. For projects with no set termination dates (for example, groundwater-monitoring networks), technical reviews will be held at least annually. Additionally, ongoing and frequent, informal reviews are conducted during team meetings, and during discussions among project staff, with the Associate Director for Hydrologic Studies, Section Chiefs, Discipline Specialists, and others, as appropriate. In some instances, technical advisory groups may be established to oversee and monitor project activities. The WAWSC Administrative Services Section maintains a file of project reviews.

WAWSC projects also receive administrative reviews (budget and timelines) approximately quarterly. The outcomes of these reviews are shared with the Associate Director for Hydrologic Studies to proactively identify potential problems in completing a study as planned. If, during the quarterly reviews or during the course of a project, it is determined that additional technical review, support, or oversight is needed, the Hydrologic Studies Program Chief and the Groundwater Specialist will schedule the review and assemble a review panel, often including reviewers and subject specialists outside the Center.

Formal Report Review Procedures

All reports written by WAWSC staff that deal with groundwater or have a significant component of groundwater hydrology will be reviewed by the Center Groundwater Specialist or a designated alternate prior to submission of the report for colleague review. This process should occur after the report has been reviewed by the appropriate author's supervisor, but may occur concurrently with the colleague review process given mutual agreement between the author, the author's supervisor, and the Center Groundwater Specialist. The Center Groundwater Specialist may request an interim review by the WSFT Groundwater Specialist if the report contains information of a new or innovative nature, or if the Center Groundwater Specialist has concerns about technical issues of the project or the subsequent report.

Formal report review procedures are outlined in detail in WAWSC internal memoranda available to Center staff via the WAWSC intranet (WAWSC 1994-06-17, WAWSC 2003-01-27, and WAWSC 2003-03-06). Authors of reports to be published within the WAWSC should familiarize themselves with the policies detailed in these policy memoranda. Response to Colleagues, Center Groundwater Specialists, Water Science Field Team Groundwater Specialists, and Bureau Approving Official review memoranda are required and should accompany the reports package submitted for USGS Bureau approval. These policies are in place to assure that all pertinent technical, policy, and editorial review comments have been addressed and to assure the technical and editorial quality of WAWSC reports.

Triennial Discipline Reviews

USGS Offices of Groundwater and Water Quality conduct Technical Reviews of the groundwater and water-quality programs in the WAWSC approximately every three years. At the time of publication of this document (2013), the most recent review was conducted in May 2013. The review team includes technical experts of the USGS Water Science Field Team, Offices of Groundwater and Water Quality, and an independent "data reviewer", usually a Discipline Specialist, DBA, or senior hydrologist/hydrologic technician from another Water Science Center (WSC) that has a strong background in data collection and processing activities.

The objectives of the triennial review are to (1) ensure that all Science Center offices produce hydrologic data and information that meet U.S. Geological Survey standards, (2) ensure that Center science practices conform to established quality-assurance guidelines, and (3) make technical recommendations and suggest sources of information to assist Center personnel in collecting and analyzing data for data programs and interpretive projects. The review also is designed to maintain technical communication among Center, Region, and Headquarters personnel in a forum that focuses on exchange of technical information among all participants.

Prior to the review, the Review Team is provided with a list of all current projects and proposals, and a list of regularly scheduled groundwater and water-quality field activities expected to take place during the period of the review. The list of projects is used to develop an effective review agenda and should include the period of investigation (beginning and ending fiscal years), project or proposal title, name of the project chief, end date, and total funding (simply to determine the relative size of the project). The list of current projects and proposals, and scheduled field activities during the review week, is used by the Water Science Field Team Specialists in coordination with Science Center staff and Review Team Leader to develop an agenda.

The review is typically conducted over a four-day period with most activities occurring in the Center office. Additionally, the groundwater data reviewer typically visits one or two wells in each field office in order to meet with a hydrologic technician and visit selected real-time wells. They will accompany the technician on a field visit to the well and will visit the office to review the data collection and records computation process. Most commonly, they review the previous water year data. They also will check for mandatory safety equipment, such as fire extinguishers, first aid kits, and traffic control equipment, if necessary. Following the review, the Review Team provides written comments to the Center summarizing the findings of their review. The Center then develops a written response outlining corrective steps that are, or will, be taken in order to address any deficiencies in approach or methodology identified by the Review Team.

It is expected that issues raised in the previous triennial discipline review will begin to be addressed as soon as practical, upon receipt of the review memo from the Office of Groundwater. To assure that all issues raised during the review are addressed prior to the next review, preferably at least a year in advance of the next review, the Center Groundwater Specialist will consult with WSC project and data-section staff involved with groundwater data collection or processing activities, to address any unresolved issues identified in the previous triennial review and make preparations for the ensuing review.

Data Collection

The objectives of the individual study will determine the types of data collected and the frequency with which data are collected. The Project Chief must clearly document and provide to the project personnel, in sufficient detail, the types and quality of data needed so that the project team can collectively determine the appropriate data-collection techniques to satisfy project objectives. Routine and non-routine data-collection activities and procedures are documented by project or support personnel and recorded in appropriate field notebooks or on approved forms. These notes and forms are to be kept with project files and archived upon project completion.

Project Chiefs are responsible for supervision of field procedures and activities and must assure, through personal observation or with the assistance of the Center Groundwater Specialist, that field personnel are adequately trained and fully qualified to collect and process data needed for the project. The Center Groundwater Specialist will review the data activities of all groundwater projects as part of periodic project reviews scheduled by the Associate Director for Hydrologic Studies. If project staff are determined to be inadequately trained to conduct their duties, the Project Chief, in consultation with the Center Groundwater Specialist and the appropriate Section or Field Office Chief will assure that project staff, receive appropriate training to ensure technical competence and to rectify inadequacies.

The Center Groundwater Specialist, or designated representative, may institute random reviews of field practices to assure data are collected according to specifications documented in this plan. Frequent random checks of recently hired or seasonal personnel are essential, but even experienced field staff would benefit from periodic review of field procedures, as new policies and procedures are added or revised over time.

All Scientists and Technicians that collect and (or) process groundwater data must be familiar with the guidelines specified in this plan to assure that technical products and reports published by the WASWSC meet all applicable Department of the Interior, USGS, OGW, WMA, and WAWSC policies.

Documentation of Technical Procedures

Procedures used for the collection of groundwater data are derived from a series of technical-procedures documents, technical memoranda, Techniques of Water-Resources Investigations (TWRIs) reports, and numerous other publications. The primary documentation of technical procedures for groundwater data-collection activities is the USGS Techniques and Method report 1-A1 "Groundwater Technical Procedures of the U.S. Geological Survey" (Cunningham and Schalk, comps., 2011). This report provides detailed, illustrated instructions for the implementation of common field methods for collecting groundwater data. WAWSC center staff are referred to this document and encouraged to download and print a copy of the report for field reference. Standards for groundwater-data collection are based on the methods outlined in that report, or in the selected references contained therein. The report can be downloaded at *http://pubs.usgs.gov/tm/1a1/*, and is updated as needed to incorporate elements that change through time. Technical procedures for data-collection not mentioned in any of the referenced documents should be discussed and planned with the WAWSC Groundwater Specialist and documented in the project files.

Techniques for the collection of groundwater samples for water-quality analysis are documented in the national field manual for the collection of water-quality data (U.S. Geological Survey, variously dated), in other TWRIs, in memoranda issued by the Office of Water Quality, and in publications containing technical guidance provided by the WAWSC Water-Quality Specialist. The WAWSC Groundwater Specialist will ensure that full coordination is arranged, and when applicable, that suitable cross training in water-quality procedures is provided.

Obtaining Permission to Use or Drill a Well on Private Property

USGS groundwater programs are largely dependent on data collected from, or available for, privately owned wells. The USGS has stringent guidelines for collecting data from private wells and for drilling wells on private property (appendix 2; OGW memoranda 03.03). WAWSC policy requires permission from land owners to access private property for the purpose of collecting water levels, conducting aquifer tests, borehole geophysical survey, surface geophysical surveys, or other routine groundwater-related field tasks. Written approval is strongly recommended, but in no case shall USGS WAWSC personnel access private property or make water-level measurements or conduct other tasks without at least verbal permission from the land owner. The owner's information, which may include the owner's name, address, and telephone number, should be obtained and logged on the well inventory form, but only the owner's name and note of verbal or written permission to access the property is entered into the GWSI database. Owner's name, address, and telephone number are considered personally identifiable information (PII) and are subject to specific policies as outlined in WAWSC Memo 2009-12-10 (available at WAWSC intranet site). At no time are WAWSC permitted to release PII, and WAWSC personnel are required to log access to PII as specified in the aforementioned memo. If WAWSC personnel need to drill wells on private property, the legal agreements in the OGW memoranda must be completed. The Groundwater Technical Procedures of the U.S. Geological Survey report (Cunningham and Schalk, 2011) is an excellent reference for many common groundwater procedures (available at *http://pubs.usgs.gov/tm/1a1/*). GWPD 15 of that report contains specific instructions and forms for completing a well on private property (Form 9-1483), obtaining permission to access private property, and to transfer a well to a third party (Form 9-3106). Transfer of a well to a third party is only permitted under certain specific conditions as outlined in OGW Memo 2003.03.

Instrumentation

QA procedures involving instrumentation will be conducted as described in Brunett and others (1997, p. 11–13) and Cunningham and Schalk (2011). Within the WAWSC, the primary instrumentation that requires QA/QC checks are steel tapes and electric tapes used to measure groundwater levels. The WAWSC will check all steel and electric tapes used by WAWSC staff no less than once every 3 years. The tapes will be checked against a calibrated reference tape, which will be used only for QA/QC procedures, and results of the field checks will be recorded in a log book. Any tape not meeting accuracy specifications of plus or minus (±) 0.02 ft-per-hundred foot of well depth will be repaired, replaced, or removed from service. Currently (2013) there is no established tape calibration procedure provided by the OGW. A groundwater-procedures document (GWPD) or other guidance is expected in the near future. In the interim, WAWSC personnel are referred to guidelines as developed by other USGS Water Science Centers available on the OGW intranet website.

Pressure transducers used to monitor water levels will be assessed by QA/QC procedures as specified by the vendor. Similar ± 0.02 ft per hundred foot of error should indicate potential problems with the instrument and any problems assessed as soon as practical. Methods and QA procedures for pressure transducers are described in Cunningham and Schalk (2011). Additionally, calibration and maintenance information of specific brands of pressure transducers are provided by the manufacturers and should be consulted.

Mandatory Entry of Water-Level Data in NWIS

USGS policy requires that all discrete water-level data collected by the USGS be stored in the Groundwater Site Inventory (GWSI) database (appendix 2: OGW Memo 92.06 and 93.03). Additionally, all time series water-level data collected by the USGS is required to be entered into ADAPS (appendix 2: OGW memo 06.01). Long-term permanent groundwater monitoring wells are required to be processed in accordance with established recommendations for continuous records processing (CRP) as outlined in WRD Policy Memorandum 2010.02 (available at *http://water.usgs.gov/admin/memo/policy/wrdpolicy10.02.html*.) Within the WAWSC, the Field Offices are proceeding toward full implementation of CRP as outlined in Memo 2010.02, which will include processing and approval of water-level records for long-term water-level monitoring wells including real time and Climate Response network wells. Water-level records for continuous records sites such as the temporary pressure transducer installations installed for interpretative projects should adopt similar CRP records processing procedures. If feasible to do so, Project Chiefs are encouraged to enter water-level data provided by cooperating agencies in NWIS. At a minimum, the quality of such data will be assured by WAWSC personnel prior to entry into NWIS, and appropriately coded in GWSI as to the source of the data.

To assist project staff in preparation of data for entry by the GWSI DBA or their alternate, the WAWSC has a published report (Lane, 2006) that establishes guidelines for coding and entering groundwater data into GWSI (available at *http://pubs.er.usgs.gov/publication/ofr20061371*). WAWSC project staff should consult this publication when filling out GWSI coding sheets for their projects. Although the report is not quite current with respect to recently added fields in GWSI, the report provides detailed instructions and guidelines for populating the general site, well construction, water-level, miscellaneous records, and geohydrologic sections of the GWSI coding form. Because the guidelines in the report (Lane, 2006) are not current, policies and requirements outlined in this GWQAP take precedence over those outlined in Lane (2006), in the rare event that there are any contradictions in policy or procedures between the two documents.

Minimum Requirements for Establishing a Site in NWIS

Project personnel are encouraged to fill out the GWSI coding sheet (appendix 1) in as much detail as possible. Office of Groundwater guidelines for minimal data are provided in appendix 2 (OGW memo 98.02). However, the WAWSC requires that personnel provide additional information when establishing sites in NWIS to provide for a more robust GWSI database. Currently, the GWSI database serves primarily as a repository for water-level data, but has the capacity to be used for many additional purposes, including documentation of well-construction information, storage of specific capacity and other hydraulic data, and documentation of hydrogeologic units for sites. These requirements are not solely for the sake of populating the database, but rather to make the data more useful for future WAWSC, regional, or national projects and data analyses. In recent years, population of the measurement-point information and hydrogeologic units in the WAWSC GWSI database as specified in Lane (2006) has not been routinely conducted. In many cases, well depths may be missing, and the interval of the well open to specific geologic strata are not routinely coded. This makes retrieval and use of the data for project purposes other than the retrieving water-level data difficult.

To provide for a more robust and useful GWSI database, WAWSC policy is to provide as much information on well depth, hydrogeologic units, general site data, and water levels as is practical. WAWSC staff are encouraged to populate the general site data, water-level data, construction hole data, construction-casing data, construction-openings data, construction measuring point data, discharge data, and geohydrologic data sections of the GWSI General Site Data coding form (Form 9-1904-A) in as much detail as possible. For wells with water-level data, completion of the water-level data and measuring-point data sections of the GWSI coding form are required. Measuring points may be established from well logs for those wells that are used only for geohydrologic reconnaissance, but actual measurement of casing stickup in the field is required for sites where field water-level measurements are made.

For those sites used in hydrogeologic framework characterization where the hydrogeologic units are known with a high degree of confidence, population of the primary aquifer codes C714 and C093, and completion of the Geohydrologic Data section of the GWSI coding sheet, is required. This may be conducted by batch-entry using SWUDS templates after initial entry of the site record, upon completion of detailed hydrogeologic framework analyses. For all wells entered into the GWSI database, a depth for the well is required (C028). All wells entered into GWSI database however, are required to populate the National Aquifer Code (C715). Every attempt should be made to determine or at a minimum estimate the well depth, including referring to well depth data on logs or by sounding the depth with a non-weighted steel tape. In rare instances, it may be difficult or impractical to determine the depth of a well. In these instances, the Project Chief in consultation with the GWSI DBA may request a waiver from the Center Groundwater Specialist to enter a well into GWSI without a well depth. The waiver will only be granted if detailed justification of why such a well is needed for a project is provided. To help facilitate the entry of complete site information, a WAWSC Instructional Memo dated July 7, 2008 (available on the WAWSC intranet site), describes the process for creating new sites, or updating site information in GWSI, that includes a technical review step by a Center database administrator or alternate prior to entry into NWIS.

Clarification—Establishment and Coding of Land Surface Datum and Measuring Points

By definition, a datum is a standard position or level that measurements are taken from, and is static and not subject to variation. Likewise, the measurement-point (MP) elevation is a static point in space, and unless the point is altered in some way, such as having the well casing cut to a shorter height or extended, it typically does not change. Upon initial visit to a well, project personnel will measure the height of the MP above land surface. The datum of the well may be established either by leveling/GPS at the time of the initial site visit, or in the office using LiDAR imagery, DEMs, or topographic maps. In the WAWSC, the MAPS software also may be used for establishing well datums and other general site information for new wells being entered into GWSI. However, the MAPS software only populates the General Site Information parts of the GWSI coding form, required Water Level, Well Construction, Measuring Point, Geohydrologic, and Miscellaneous sections of the form must be manually coded.

WAWSC policy is to reference all water levels in relation to land surface, so the datum for the well is the altitude of the land surface at the well (C016 on the GWSI coding sheet). Project personnel are required to document the MP from which any water level measurement is made, except for water levels that are reported and must be recorded as such in field C239 of the Water-Level Data section on the GWSI coding form. Measuring-point information will be described in detail in field C324 on the GWSI coding sheet and also on the field well inventory form. Project staff also will establish the MP height for the well (C323 on GWSI coding sheet), usually the top edge of the well casing, or the shelf of the recorder floor if the site is instrumented for long-term water-level monitoring. The beginning date for new MPs is also required and will be coded in field C321 on the GWSI coding form. If subsequent MPs are established for a well (for example, if the casing was extended, shortened, or a well shelter installed), a new MP height (C323) will be established and the MP remarks field (C324) will be used to describe the new MP. The ending date for the old MP and the beginning date for the new MP will be coded in fields C322 and C321, respectively, on the GWSI coding form; with the appropriate sequence number (C728).

If the well is surveyed to establish the datum (usually only for long-term network wells), project staff also will document the altitude of the MP, method with which altitude was determined, measuring point-altitude accuracy, and measuring point-altitude datum (C325, C326, C327, and C328 on the GWSI coding sheet). Note that the difference between the altitude of the MP (C325) and the MP height (C323) must be equivalent to the altitude for the well (C016).

Once established, the MP height will be used on subsequent visits to the well to make water-level measurements. Except for unusual and rare instances, even if the ground surface around the well is altered slightly, either by having the land surface graded or fill placed around the casing, the land surface datum has already been established and typically remains unchanged. Under most situations, land surface datums and MP heights should not be altered. This is particularly true in situations where the amount of disturbance of material around the well is minimal, and the accuracy of determination of the altitude of the well was from a map or DEM with an altitude accuracy error of several feet or more.

One notable exception is where the land surface altitude and the MP altitude have been surveyed with a high degree of accuracy and the MP height has been significantly altered (for example, if the well casing were extended, or a well shelter and recording instrumentation was placed on the well). Examples of typical coding of GWSI Coding sheets follow. For long-term water-level monitoring wells, such as wells in the NAWQA network or WAWSC water-level network (climate response, long-term, or real time) wells, surveys are required and a minimum of two independent reference marks (RMs) established to re-establish the well in the event that the measuring point is destroyed or damaged, or to document possible land subsidence around the well. The process for establishing RMs is documented in groundwater procedure document number 3 (GWPD3) of Cunningham and Schalk (2011, p. 20–23).

Example A: On July 2, 1982, an inventory of a well indicated a casing stickup (MP height) of 1.35-ft above land surface. The MP, the top edge of the steel casing, was marked with three hacksaw marks. The altitude of the land surface was determined from a topographic map with a contour interval of 40 ft to be approximately 1,705-ft above the North American Vertical Datum of 1988. The following fields should be coded on the GWSI coding sheet (form 9-1904-A):

C16 (altitude)=1,705 ft
C18 (altitude accuracy)=20 ft (half the contour interval of the topographic quadrangle)
C17 (altitude method)=N (for DEM)
C22 (altitude datum)=NAVD 88 (North American Vertical Datum of 1988)
C323 (M.P. height)=1.35 ft
C324 (M.P. remarks)=MP is top edge of steel casing marked with three hacksaw marks, 1.35-ft above land surface
C728 (record sequence No.)=001 (this is the initial MP established for this site)
C321 (beginning date)=07-02-1982
C322 (ending date)=Leave blank if site is active and MP still in use

Example B: On June 1, 1985, an inventory of a well with no readily accessible point for measuring water levels other than a vent hole drilled in the side of the casing, which is 1.50 ft above the base of the concrete well pad, indicated that the well pad is poured to a height of 0.40 ft above land surface. In this case, the MP height will be 1.90 ft, as WAWSC policy is to reference all water levels to land surface. Additionally, the altitude of land surface at the well, and the altitude of the MP of the well were determined to within 0.01 ft accuracy by RTK GPS to be 1,406.24 and 1,408.14 ft above the

North American Vertical Datum of 1988, respectively. The following fields should be coded on the GWSI coding sheet:

C16 (altitude of Site)=1,406.24 ft
C18 (altitude accuracy for Land Surface)=0.01 ft
C17 (altitude method for Land Surface)=D (for DGPS)
C22 (altitude datum for Land Surface)=NAVD 88 (North American Vertical Datum of 1988)
C323 (M.P. height)=1.90 ft
C325 (altitude of measuring point)=1,408.14 (altitude of land surface + M.P. height)
C324 (M.P. remarks)=M.P. is vent hole in side of well casing marked with red paint, 1.50 above
        base of concrete well pad and 1.90-ft above land surface
C728 (record sequence No.)=001 (this is the initial M.P. established for this site)
C321 (Beginning date for MP)=06-01-1985
C322 (Ending date for MP)=leave blank if site is active and M.P. still in use
C326 (altitude method for MP)=D (for DGPS)
C327 (altitude accuracy for MP)=0.01 ft
C328 (altitude datum for MP)=NAVD 88 (North American Vertical Datum of 1988)

Example C: From Example B above, the pump was removed on May 15, 2011, the casing was extended, and a logger, a DCP, and a shelter were installed on the well. The well was re-surveyed before and after installation of the logger, DCP, and shelter. The elevation of the new MP from optical levels was determined to be exactly 1.270 ft higher than the old MP (vent hole in side of casing). The vent hole in the casing was welded shut to prevent inadvertent use of the old MP. The following fields should be coded on the GWSI coding sheet:

C728 (record sequence No.)=001 (to enter end date for initial M.P.)
C322 (ending date for old M.P.)=05-15-2011
C728 (record sequence No.)=002 (this is the second MP established for the well)
C16 (altitude)=Not needed; the altitude (datum) for the well was previously established to a high
        degree of accuracy by RTK GPS survey and does not require updating
C323 (M.P. height)=3.17 ft (original M.P. height of 1.90 ft + additional 1.27 ft due to extension
        of casing and installation of recorder shelter)
C325 (altitude of measuring point)=1,409.41 (altitude of land surface+new M.P. height)
C324 (M.P. remarks)=MP is top edge of recorder shelter floor, 2.77-ft above base of concrete
        well pad and 3.17-ft above land surface.
C321 (beginning date for new M.P.)=05-15-2011
C322 (ending date for new M.P.)=leave blank for site is active and new MP in use
C326 (altitude method for M.P.)=L (for level or other surveying instrument)
C327 (altitude accuracy for M.P.)=0.01 ft
C328 (altitude datum for M.P.)=NAVD 88 (North American Vertical Datum of 1988)
For record, sequence number 001 from example C, the end date for the initial MP was changed to 05-15-2011, as the vent hole was welded shut and no longer available for use as of that date. Although it would be possible to have two or more MPs (not welding the vent hole shut), it is not advisable unless necessary, because it provides the opportunity for confusion and unintentional use of multiple MPs.

MONKES – Mandatory use of MONKES for long-term water-level networks

The OGW encourages use of the Multi Optional Network Key Entry System (MONKES) program for collection of water-level data (appendix 2; OGW memo 06.02). The MONKES software offers several enhanced features which help assure the quality of water-level data collected in the field. First, the software stores the field water-level measurements and does logic checks of the math for water-level computations. The software also automatically time stamps the measurements with date and time of measurement. Past measurements are stored on the personal data assistant (PDA) used to collect the water-level data, so field personnel can assess whether the water-level measurements made are consistent with past measurements. Finally and most importantly, the software prepares the data for entry into the GWSI database, thereby saving time on data entry and eliminating the potential for transcription errors possible with manual entry of water level data.

For these reasons, WAWSC policy is that the MONKES software shall be used for collection of all water-level data collected from long-term water-level monitoring networks; which includes the OGW sponsored federal index wells, climate response network (CRN) wells, and the real-time water-level network. In addition, monthly, annual, or semi-annual water-level networks established in support of WAWSC groundwater projects are also required to use the MONKES software for collection and download of routine water-level data. MONKES is not required for use where only one or two water-level measurements are made, such as occurs during well inventories.

Two files are generated by the MONKES software, a GWSI input file for updating the water levels in the GWSI database and an XML file. The XML file should be parsed by site using the site visit generator software available on the MONKES intranet website. The XML file is considered original record and shall be stored in a permanent computer archive. The GWSI input file generated shall also be filed and kept as part of current water-year work record, but is not considered permanent record and therefore does not necessarily have to be permanently archived.

Current WAWSC policy is to also record all water-level measurements on an accepted water-level note sheet. Two water-level note sheets have been approved for use in the WAWSC (appendix 2) for recording and documenting water-level measurements. This requirement is for all network and long-term project wells. The only exception is for initial water-level measurements made during synoptic well inventories, in which case it is acceptable to record the initial water-level measurements made as part of well inventory on the WAWSC well inventory form.

The policy to record water-level measurements on approved note sheets and in MONKES may be waived in the future, but at present and until advised by the Center Groundwater Specialist, for long-term or project network wells, water-levels shall be recorded both in MONKES and on an approved WAWSC water-level note sheet (appendix 1).

Groundwater data within the WAWSC are collected and processed by two primary groups, as part of interpretative projects, and as part of basic data activities Field Offices of the WAWSC. Data processing, storage, and archival processes are well established as part of basic data programs in the Field Offices, and questions related to the collection, processing, storage, and archival of groundwater data in the Field Offices should be referred to the appropriate Field Office Chief in consultation with the Center Groundwater Specialist, GWSI DBA, and the Assistant Director for Hydrologic Data.

For interpretative projects, however, policies and procedures related to the collection, storage, processing, and archiving of groundwater data are not well established. Currently (2013), the WAWSC Data Structure Committee is in the process of developing policies and procedures for processing, storage, and archival of both paper and electronic data. The committee's oversight is primarily for interpretative projects, but also considers policies and procedures used by the Field Offices as part of basic data programs to assure that common policies and procedures apply to both groups. The committee has not yet completed its work, and therefore has not fully developed policies and procedures for processing, storage, and archival of paper and electronic data within the WAWSC. In the interim, personnel should consult with the Center Groundwater Specialist and the GWSI DBA on the most recent storage, archiving, and data processing policies and procedures as they relate to interpretative groundwater projects.

Station Descriptions and Job Hazard Analyses (JHAs)

For long-term established water-level monitoring sites, such as the WAWSC's Real-Time and Climate Response Network wells, or for long-term monthly, quarterly, or periodic interpretative project network wells, station descriptions and JHAs are required to be developed and stored in office folders or in electronic format in a directory in the field office or recommended Data committee data structure. A copy of the station description and JHA will also be kept on site at the well (if the well has an enclosure or shelter). If the well does not have a shelter or enclosure, then a copy of the station description and JHA will be kept in the field folder, or alternatively in a directory structure on the servicing personnel's PDA. Such information will provide individuals servicing the site with pertinent information on measuring points, reference marks for re-establishing the well MP if it is damaged, safety and hazard considerations, and past water-level measurements for assessing trends and determining approximate target level when making water-level measurements. Much of this information is also available to field personnel as part of data entered into the MONKES software.

Well Integrity Tests

For long-term, established water-level monitoring sites, such as the WAWSC's Real-Time and Climate Response Network wells, periodic well-integrity tests are required to assure the wells are in hydraulic communication with the aquifer, and that the well has not been damaged or collapsed. An OGW memoranda (appendix 2: OGW memo 12.01) describes the types of acceptable well-integrity tests. Well-integrity tests shall be conducted on a 3- to 5-year basis, or when it is suspected that there are problems with the well. If access to the well is suitable for a total depth (sounding) measurement, the depth of the well shall be checked annually to assure that the well has not collapsed. The Center Groundwater Specialist should be notified if the overall depth of the well cannot be verified as part of the annual total-depth measurement. If the recorded depth of the well has changed significantly, or the depth indicates that the effective open-screen length has decreased significantly, then well integrity could be compromised, and additional testing and/or well maintenance may be necessary.

Surveying of Well Datums

The USGS OGW requires that all wells used for routine, long-term water-level measurements be surveyed or leveled to provide for re-establishment of the well datum in the event of damage to the well, land subsidence, or change in the well datum or measuring point. For long-term, established water-level monitoring sites, such as the WAWSC's Real-Time and Climate Response Network wells, periodic (about once every 3–5 years) levels of wells shall be conducted. The levels are necessary to document the datum for the well and subsequent water levels. This is important in the event that the well is damaged or vandalized. Other considerations such as land subsidence or movement in ground surface resulting from earthquakes can also alter the land surface and affect the datum of the well. Because all water levels are referenced to a land-surface datum, it is imperative that the datum can be re-established should the well be damaged or ground-surface near the well is affected. In addition to establishing the elevation of the measuring point, two independent reference marks are required from which the measuring point may be re-established should the well be damaged or altered. A complete station level circuit should be completed as specified in USGS Techniques and Methods report 3-A19 (available at *http://pubs.usgs.gov/tm/tm3A19/*), which outlines procedures for conducting levels at gaging stations and wells (Kenney, T.A., 2010). The Station Levels software which is pre-loaded field software on Hydrologic Instrumentation Facility (HIF) supplied PDAs is particularly useful for helping to collect, process, and store station levels in proper format. Specific policies and procedures for periodic station levels at long-term monitoring wells are outlined in OGW groundwater procedures document (GWPD3) as outlined in Cunningham and Schalk (2011).

Additionally, where bench marks are not found near a well, survey-grade GPS instruments are particularly useful for helping to establish datums for wells, and tying the datum into the National Vertical Datum of 1988 (NAVD 88) and the North American horizontal Datum of 1983 (NAD 83). NAVD 88 and NAD 83 are the preferred datums that should be used for establishing new wells. GPS units used for well inventories should be set to these datums prior to conducting synoptic well inventories.

Data Processing, Review, Storage, and Archiving

All groundwater data and associated reports and databases will be processed, reviewed, stored, and archived in accordance with applicable Department of the Interior (DOI), USGS, WRD, WMA, OGW or WAWSC instructional memoranda on said topics. This includes the formal report review processes and archival of aquifer tests, numerical flow models, borehole logs, GIS, and surface geophysical data.

Entry of Sites in GWSI

According to WAWSC policy, routine creation and entry of sites into the Groundwater Site Inventory (GWSI) database is the responsibility of the GWSI database administrator (DBA). Three additional individuals also have write access to the (GWSI) database, and serve as backups in the event that the DBA is unavailable to enter sites for an extended period of time (WAWSC intranet site; memorandum 2008-07-07). The only notable exception for having sites entered by one of the backup DBAs is for sites that need to be entered expeditiously during the DBA's absence to avoid associated analytical results being rejected by the National Water Quality Laboratory due to the lack of an appropriate site file being established in the database. However, proper planning and coordination should eliminate the need for the alternate DBAs to enter sites into the site file except under the most adverse of situations. If a minimal site file should be required for entry into GWSI by an alternate DBA, then a full documentation of the site should follow as soon as practical, and coordinated with the primary GWSI DBA. This policy is in effect to prevent minimal or poorly documented site file entry into GWSI, and to provide for rigorous QA/QC of water-level data and sites being entered in GWSI.

Additionally, Project Chiefs are required to consult with the Center GWSI DBA and Groundwater Specialist prior to initiation of large-scale synoptic well, spring, or stream inventories. The purpose of the consultation is to assure that sufficient time is allocated and scheduled for entry of sites and water-level data into the GWSI database. Project Chiefs must also assure that sufficient funding is available to account for the time required to properly code GWSI coding sheets, and to enter sites and/or water-level data into the GWSI database. Several individuals in the WAWSC have experience coding

GWSI forms, but it is important that Project Chiefs coordinate with the Center Groundwater Specialist or GWSI DBA if they require assistance with the coding of GWSI forms, so that arrangements can be made with the section chiefs to allocate personnel to GWSI coding and site/water level entry tasks.

Aquifer Test Archives

Office of Groundwater policy (appendix 2; OGW memoranda 94.02 and 09.01) requires that all aquifer tests conducted by the USGS be archived for future retrieval. Projects within the WAWSC for which aquifer tests are conducted are required to receive regional approval of the tests by the WSFT Groundwater Specialist, and to archive that data in a long-term digital aquifer test archive. Specifications for Office of Groundwater requirements for the aquifer test archives are presented in appendix 2. Project staff shall coordinate with the Center Groundwater Specialist on the archiving of aquifer test data.

Groundwater Model Archives

Office of Groundwater policy (appendix 2; OGW memoranda 11.01) requires that all groundwater models be approved by the WSFT Groundwater Specialists. Specifications for OGW requirements for documentation and development of numerical groundwater flow and solute transport models are presented in appendix 2. Project staff involved with development of numerical groundwater flow models should review and be aware of the requirements of USGS policy for archiving groundwater flow models. Project Chiefs must be able to satisfy the requirement that the models can run independently of any graphical user (GUI), third party, or in-house software used to develop the models, using standard USGS codes. If modeling codes other than USGS software are used, archiving of the software and models should be coordinated with the WSFT Groundwater Specialists. Such software must be archived for future use if the GUI is based originally on the use of USGS software. Upon completion of this process, project personnel shall coordinate with the Center Groundwater Specialist on the archiving of numerical groundwater flow and solute transport models in the WAWSC Groundwater Model Archive.

Borehole Geophysical Data Archives

Office of Groundwater policy (appendix 2; OGW memoranda 00.03 and 10.01) requires that all borehole geophysical data collected by the USGS be archived for future retrieval. Future projects within the WAWSC collecting borehole geophysics data are required to archive that data in a long-term digital borehole geophysics archive. Specifications for OGW requirements for the borehole geophysics archives are presented in appendix 2 (OGW Memos 00.03 and 10.01). Project staff shall coordinate with the Center Groundwater Specialist on archival of borehole geophysical data.

Surface Geophysical Data Archives

Office of Groundwater policy (appendix 2; OGW memoranda 09.02) requires that all surface geophysical data collected by the USGS be archived for future retrieval. Fiber optic distributed temperature sensor (DTS) data collected routinely by the WAWSC are considered surface geophysical data and must be archived according to specifications detailed in for OGW Memo 09.02 (appendix 2). Should WAWSC staff begin to collect additional types of surface geophysics data in support of groundwater projects, then that data also must be archived in accordance with specification in OGW

Memo 09.02. Project staff shall coordinate with the Center Groundwater Specialist on archival of surface geophysical data.

Archiving Project/GIS Information

WAWSC has specific policies for archiving of project data and GIS databases (WAWSC intranet site; memoranda WAWSC 2008-08-13 a, b, and c). These archives are important in the event that the validity or interpretations of data in approved USGS reports are questioned. The archive is required to serve as a repository of important project information should it be necessary to review an issue or reproduce information published in USGS reports. It is also important as future studies in the same geographic area often make use of previously collected data. Refer to WAWSC policy for archiving of project data and GIS information (including creation of GIS metadata). Project staff should coordinate with the WAWSC GIS Specialist on archiving and documentation of GIS data.

Summary

This quality-assurance plan documents the standards, policies, and procedures used by the U.S. Geological Survey's (USGS) Washington Water Science Center (WAWSC), for activities related to the collection, processing, storage, analysis, and publication of groundwater data. This plan serves as a guide to all WAWSC personnel involved in groundwater activities, and changes as the needs and requirements of the WAWSC, the USGS, and the Water Resources Mission Area evolve. The plan is based largely on requirements and guidelines from the USGS Office of Groundwater, or from the USGS Water Resources Mission Area. Regular updates to this plan represent an integral part of the quality-assurance process. This report supplants, and is an amendment and a substantial update to the previous groundwater QA plan (Drost, 2005). This updated plan includes information related to organization and responsibilities of WAWSC personnel, training, safety, development of project proposals, project review procedures, data collection activities, data processing activities, report review procedures, and archival of field data and interpretative information pertaining to groundwater-flow models, borehole aquifer tests, and aquifer tests.

As with all quality assurance documents, this groundwater assurance plan is a living document, and subject to periodic updates. Technology changes rapidly, and new procedures to deal with demands of evolving technology are commonly required. Additionally, the USGS Office of Groundwater periodically releases policy requirements that need to be incorporated in the groundwater quality-assurance plan.

Important updates from the previous groundwater assurance plan include: (1) procedures for documenting and archiving groundwater-flow models; (2) revisions to procedures and policies for creation of sites in the Groundwater Site Inventory database (GWSI); (3) dissemination of new water-level forms to be used within the WAWSC; (4) procedures for future creation of borehole geophysics, surface geophysics, and aquifer test archives, and; (5) use of the USGS Multi Optional Network Key Entry System (MONKES) software for collection and entry of routine water-level data collected as part of long-term water-level monitoring networks.

The report also includes the more relevant USGS, USGS Office of Groundwater, and Water Resources Discipline or Water Mission Area policy and instructional memoranda from which the requirements within this plan are based. Groundwater procedure documents (GWPDs) are an important resource for reference to established USGS policies and procedures.

References Cited

Brunett, J.O., Barber, N.L., Burns, A.W., Fogelman, R.P., Gillies, D.C., Lidwin, R.A., and Mack, T.J., 1997, A quality-assurance plan for district ground-water activities of the U.S. Geological Survey: U.S. Geological Survey Open-File Report 97-11. (Also available at *http://water.usgs.gov/ogw/pubs/OFR9711/index.html*.)

Cunningham, W.L., and Schalk, C.W., comps., 2011, Groundwater technical procedures of the U.S. Geological Survey: U.S. Geological Survey Techniques and Methods 1–A1, 151 p. (Also available at *http://pubs.usgs.gov/tm/1a1/*.)

Drost, B.W., 2005, Quality-assurance plan for ground-water activities, U.S. Geological Survey, Washington Water Science Center: U.S. Geological Survey Open-File Report 2005-1126, 27 p. (Also available at *http://pubs.usgs.gov/of/2005/1126/*.)

Kenney, T.A., 2010, Levels at gaging stations: U.S. Geological Survey Techniques and Methods 3-A19, 60 p. (Also available at *http://pubs.usgs.gov/tm/tm3A19/*.)

Lane, R.C., 2006, Guidelines for coding and entering ground-water data into the ground-water site inventory database version 4.6, U.S. Geological Survey Washington Water Science Center: U.S. Geological Survey Open-File Report 2006-1371, 104 p. (Also available at *http://pubs.er.usgs.gov/publication/ofr20061371*.)

Schroder, L.J., and Shampine, W.J., 1992, Guidelines for preparing a quality-assurance plan for district offices of the U.S. Geological Survey: U.S. Geological Survey Open-File Report 92-136, 14 p. (Also available at *http://pubs.er.usgs.gov/publication/ofr92136*.)

Shampine, W.L., Pope, L.M., and Koterba, M.T., 1992, Integrating quality assurance in project work plans of the U.S. Geological Survey: U.S. Geological Survey Open-File Report 92-162, 12 p. Also available at *http://pubs.er.usgs.gov/publication/ofr92162*.)

U.S. Geological Survey, variously dated, National field manual for the collection of water-quality data: U.S. Geological Survey Techniques of Water-Resources Investigations, book 9, chaps. A1–A9, (Also available at *http://pubs.water.usgs.gov/twri9A*.)

Appendix 1. Standard Forms for USGS Washington Water Science Center use

Groundwater Coding Forms

The standard groundwater (GW) coding forms used by Washington Water Science Center (WAWSC) personnel are routinely updated by the National Water Information System (NWIS) based on new requirements of the Groundwater Site Inventory GWSI Database. Current forms are available on the USGS NWIS intranet website.

WAWSC personnel should download the most recent version of the appropriate coding form, GW coding form—General site data for wells, SW—Site data coding form for surface-water sites, and GW coding form—General Spring Data for springs. These forms are also routinely downloaded by the Center Groundwater Specialist and may be obtained from the Center Groundwater Specialist by request.

Water-Level Field Forms

The standard water-level field forms provided for use by NWIS in the past are not applicable for use by current standards. This is primarily due to the addition of new mandatory requirements for water-level data required for entry into GWSI. As a result, common practice is for USGS Water Science Centers to develop their own water-level field forms. At the time of publication of this Groundwater Quality Assurance Plan (2013), multiple types of field forms were in use by Center Staff, none of which met current USGS specifications. This lack of standardization in field forms adds additional time to the records review process, and may result in missing or incomplete field data. WAWSC policy is that all water level measurements must specify the date of the measurement, initials of field personnel making the measurement, the type of tape used (steel tape or electric tape), and the complete water-level measurement. For water-levels measured using a steel tape, the initial mark held, the wet line mark, the depth to water, the land surface datum (LSD) measuring point (MP) correction, and the final water level must all be recorded. It is not acceptable to record only the depth to water. All calculations must be shown on the form.

To assure that all appropriate data are recorded, the WAWSC has approved two field forms for use by WAWSC staff. The first form is a modification of Form 9-1904-E (Form 9-1904-E-2012), which is commonly referred to as the "Christmas Tree Form", due to its red and green text format, and is widely used in the WAWSC. This form was modified to add the time field now required by NWIS. Form 9-1904-E-2012 is not approved for field use, only for archiving of water-level measurements in the office. The second is a standard 5 x 8 inch field form (Form WAWSC-2012), which has been developed to include all the necessary data currently required by NWIS. Form WAWSC-2012 is the only form accepted for field use in the WAWSC.

Form 9-1904-E
Revised by WA WSC March 2012

SITE ID NO.

U.S. DEPARTMENT OF THE INTERIOR
Geological Survey
WATER RESOURCES DIVISION
WATER-LEVEL DATA

WELL NUMBER

OTHER ID

M.P. HEIGHT

DATE	709 = TIME (Local)	237 = WATER LEVEL (BELOW LSD)	STATUS	METHOD	HOLD	CUT	DEPTH BELOW MP	REMARKS	PERSON MAKING VISIT	DATE ENTERED
235 # / /	709 =	237 =	238 =	239 =						
235 # / /	709 =	237 =	238 =	239 =						
235 # / /	709 =	237 =	238 =	239 =						
235 # / /	709 =	237 =	238 =	239 =						
235 # / /	709 =	237 =	238 =	239 =						
235 # / /	709 =	237 =	238 =	239 =						
235 # / /	709 =	237 =	238 =	239 =						
235 # / /	709 =	237 =	238 =	239 =						
235 # / /	709 =	237 =	238 =	239 =						
235 # / /	709 =	237 =	238 =	239 =						
235 # / /	709 =	237 =	238 =	239 =						
235 # / /	709 =	237 =	238 =	239 =						
235 # / /	709 =	237 =	238 =	239 =						
235 # / /	709 =	237 =	238 =	239 =						
235 # / /	709 =	237 =	238 =	239 =						
235 # / /	709 =	237 =	238 =	239 =						
235 # / /	709 =	237 =	238 =	239 =						
235 # / /	709 =	237 =	238 =	239 =						
235 # / /	709 =	237 =	238 =	239 =						
235 # / /	709 =	237 =	238 =	239 =						
235 # / /	709 =	237 =	238 =	239 =						
235 # / /	709 =	237 =	238 =	239 =						
235 # / /	709 =	237 =	238 =	239 =						
235 # / /	709 =	237 =	238 =	239 =						
235 # / /	709 =	237 =	238 =	239 =						

METHOD OF MEASUREMENT 239 =

	A	B	C	E	F	G	H	L	M	N	R	S	T	U	V	Z
	Airline Analog	Cali-brated Airline	Estimated	Trans-ducer	Pressure Gage	Calibrated Pressure Gage	Geo-physical Logs	Manometer	Non-recording Gage	Reported	Steel Tape	Electric Tape	Un-known	Calibrated Electric Tape	Other

SITE STATUS 238 =

	A	B	D	E	F	G	H	I	J	N	P	R	S	T	V	W	X	Z
	Atmos-pheric Pressure	Tide Stage	Dry	Recently Flowing	Flowing	Nearby Recently Flowing	Nearby Flowing	Injector	Nearby Injector	Discon-tinued	Obstruc-tion	Pump-ing	Recently Pumping	Nearby Pumping	Recently Pumped	Well Destroyed	Affected by Surface-Water Site	Foreign Matter	Other

M.P. Begin Date 321 # / /

M.P. End Date 322 = / /

M.P. Height 323 =

M.P. Remark 324 =

24

USGS — science for a changing world

U.S. DEPARTMENT OF THE INTERIOR
U.S. Geological Survey
Washington Water Science Center
WELL VISIT FORM

PROJECT: _____

Station ID: _____ Date: _____

Local Number: _____ Party: _____

Measure Point (MP): _____ above/below land surface

MP description:

Time					
*T / S / other					
Hold					
Cut					
WL below MP					
MP					
WL – MP					
**Status					

*METHOD = T: electric tape, S: steel Tape, R: reported

**STATUS= P:pumping, R:recently pumped F: flowing,B: tidal, S: nearby pumping, blank is static

Transducer Present?   YES   NO
Initial transducer reading: _____
Time: _____ Local or UTC

Data Downloaded?   YES   NO
Date: _____
File Name: _____

Tranducer RESET?   YES   NO
Date: _____
Time: _____
WL value reset to: _____
New log name: _____

REMARKS: _____
_____
_____
_____

USGS — science for a changing world

U.S. DEPARTMENT OF THE INTERIOR
U.S. Geological Survey
Washington Water Science Center
WELL VISIT FORM

PROJECT: _____

Station ID: _____ Date: _____

Local Number: _____ Party: _____

Measure Point (MP): _____ above/below land surface

MP description:

Time					
*T / S / other					
Hold					
Cut					
WL below MP					
MP					
WL – MP					
**Status					

*METHOD = T: electric tape, S: steel Tape, R: reported

**STATUS= P:pumping, R:recently pumped F: flowing,B: tidal, S: nearby pumping, blank is static

Transducer Present?   YES   NO
Initial transducer reading: _____
Time: _____ Local or UTC

Data Downloaded?   YES   NO
Date: _____
File Name: _____

Tranducer RESET?   YES   NO
Date: _____
Time: _____
WL value reset to: _____
New log name: _____

REMARKS: _____
_____
_____
_____

Appendix 2. Pertinent Technical Memoranda

Index of Technical Memoranda

October 12, 2012

WATER MISSION AREA MEMORANDUM NO. 13.01

Subject: Programs and Plans-Guidelines for Preparation, Submission, and Approval of Water Science Center Project Proposals

This memorandum establishes a consistent set of guidelines for the preparation, submission, and approval of project proposals to the Water Mission Area. Project proposals serve to focus, coordinate, communicate, and document USGS science activities. Because the proposal specifies the scope and objectives, approach, timeline and expected products it provides a basis for evaluating project progress and success and aids in ensuring cooperator satisfaction. Formal reviews of proposed projects help to ensure adherence to all applicable technical and organizational policy issues (including alignment with Bureau priorities) for reimbursable, Cooperative Water Program (CWP), and Other Federal Agency (OFA) water-resources projects. Prior to initiating the formal proposal process, Science Centers are encouraged to informally discuss proposed water-resources project concepts with appropriate Water Science Field Team (WSFT) personnel, the Regional Science Advisor and/or Safety Officer.

PREPARATION OF PROJECT PROPOSALS BY WATER SCIENCE CENTERS

Project proposals are mandatory for interpretive projects and may be required for data projects. Generally, a project can be defined as: a set of related activities or planned efforts designed to achieve a definite goal (or set of goals) with specified staff, budget and time requirements appropriate to the nature of the work, and that culminates with measurable products, services, or results. The types of activities that typically require the development, review, and approval of a project proposal include:

☐☐ All interpretive activities,

☐☐ Data activities that have a defined set of objectives and scope and data-quality objectives that rely on non-standard methods, and

☐☐ Data-collection projects that grow substantially in scope or are planned from the start to address a set of objectives that will involve interpretive work.

Specific requirements for proposal preparation are outlined in Attachment 1. Approved draft proposals are posted on the internal USGS WSFT web site at (*http://water.usgs.gov/usgs/wsft/proposals.html*). These approved draft proposals and can be used as examples.

SUBMISSION OF PROJECT PROPOSALS TO THE WATER SCIENCE FIELD TEAM

Project proposals must be submitted to the WSFT for review of technical and policy considerations to ensure that projects are technically sound and meet national quality standards; projects have an approved outlet for data, scientific information and interpretation; and the work does not violate USGS policy. If unexpected technical findings or fiscal circumstances result in significant modification of planned project activities and funding levels, a revised proposal must be submitted for review and approval by the WSFT and the Regional Director's (RD) Office.

Similarly, a new proposal will be required when data collection projects, for which no proposal was originally required, transition into interpretive studies.

The WSFT will be issuing unified guidance on proposal submissions and will institute a single proposal tracking system and repository during Fiscal Year 2013. Until then, proposals should be submitted according to past practice of the WSFT serving your Region.

APPROVAL OF PROJECT PROPOSALS BY THE REGIONAL DIRECTOR

After project proposals are reviewed by the WSFT for technical and policy considerations, a recommendation for approval will be sent to the appropriate Regional Director's Office. Final approval of the project proposal is the responsibility of the RD Office. Project work should not begin without RD Office approval, a signed Joint Funding Agreement, and entry of the project into BASIS+. (Note: A waiver to begin work without a signed agreement with appropriate justification may be submitted to the RD Office for approval. Time-sensitive activities, such as those associated with floods or emergencies, may also proceed with verbal approval from the RD Office.)

If you have questions regarding the preparation, submission, or approval of project proposals, please contact the appropriate WSFT Chief for your Science Center.

William H. Werkheiser *//s// William H. Werkheiser*

Associate Director for Water

DISTRIBUTION: A, B, RD Offices, WSCs

Attachments:

1. Guidelines For Preparation Of Project Proposals
2. Strengthening the Relevance and Benefits Section of Proposals

Attachment 1

GUIDELINES FOR PREPARATION OF PROJECT PROPOSALS

It is vitally important that USGS science be relevant to the strategic directions, and priorities of the Bureau, Water Mission Area (WMA), and Regions. Additionally, it is critical that we communicate to our stakeholders the specific needs or problems to be addressed and the science objectives and approaches of the proposed studies. A well formulated, scientifically sound project proposal is essential to the success of a project and forms the basis for effective communication of our planned and ongoing science activities. Other important functions of a good project proposal include:

☐☐ Documents the appropriateness to the USGS mission and priorities.

☐☐ Facilitates successful planning and execution of the project by describing the objectives and scope of work envisioned as well as the proposed methodologies and products (deliverables). The proposal thus serves as a list of the agreed upon commitments that can be used to gauge the successful completion of the project.

☐☐ Specifies the amount and sources of funding needed to execute the project.

Guidelines for developing pre-proposals and full proposals are described below in terms of their content, submission, review and approval. The following points summarize the intent and expectations for pre-proposals and full proposals.

Pre-proposals (*Optional*):

☐☐ Can be informal brief 'draft' idea/concept statements that outline prospective projects. Pre-proposals are *optional*, but early consultation with the Water Science Field Team (WSFT) may result in faster turn-around times when the full proposal is submitted. Content and format are flexible. Typically, the pre-proposal will include a brief background or problem statement, a list of primary objectives, discussion of the approach envisioned to achieve the stated objectives, and preliminary report/product plans.

☐☐ Submit directly to the appropriate WSFT personnel and similarly to the Regional Science Advisor and Safety Officer, as appropriate. The WSFT will provide informal timely comments on the technical or policy aspects of the preproposal (turnaround time for WSFT review of pre-proposals generally will be less than one week).

Full proposal (*approval required*):

Concise but thorough narratives should address each of the required elements **B1–B12** listed below. There is no length criterion for full proposals. Proposals may adopt a format required by the cooperator or program coordinator, as long as the required elements of the proposal are presented. In these cases, please indicate the need for a different format on the cover sheet.

☐☐ Proposals must be submitted electronically to the appropriate WSFT Chief (preferably compiled in a single file). Either PDF- or WORD-formatted versions are acceptable; any supporting figures and tables cited in the text should be embedded in the digital document. The submission must include a Project Proposal Cover Sheet (see item **A** below, and a Job Hazard Analysis with appropriate signatures.

☐☐ The WSFT review will focus on elements **B1–B8**, but the review will consider the contents of elements **B9–B11**. Element **1C**, pertaining to Safety and the Proposal Job Hazard Analysis, will be formally reviewed by the Regional Safety Officer.

☐☐ The WSFT will attempt to complete reviews of the final draft of the proposal within two weeks. The WSFT will attempt to resolve any problems with the proposals directly with the Water Science Center (WSC).

☐☐ The WSFT review package and recommendation will be sent via email to the appropriate designee in the RD Office for review and approval, with a copy to the originating WSC Director.

☐☐ The WSFT will archive approved proposals and review packages in an accessible proposal repository (currently at: *http://water.usgs.gov/usgs/wsft/proposals.html*).

Elements of a Full Proposal:

A. **A completed and signed Project Proposal Cover Sheet** (available at *http://water.usgs.gov/usgs/wsft/proposals/coversheet-template.pdf*)

B. **Project Proposal:**

1. **TITLE**—should relate, as concisely as possible, to the objective(s) and scope of the proposed study and include the location of the study, if applicable. Ideally, the title should reflect the preliminary title(s) of any proposed information product from the study. Omit company or trademarked product names in the title.

2. **BACKGROUND/INTRODUCTION**—This section can be used to provide additional information about the study area, such as demographics and political considerations, previous investigations and results, and any information that will help the reader understand the **problem** and **objective** sections of the proposal.

3. **PROBLEM**—State concisely the problems and related background information motivating USGS involvement. Note that the cooperator's problem can be described as well, but not to the exclusion of the broader water resources issue/problem. Previous studies and existing information should be briefly summarized and referenced. Provide sufficient supporting background information to facilitate understanding key technical and social factors relevant to the proposed study. For place studies, a map showing the location and extent of the study area should be included in this section.

4. **OBJECTIVES and SCOPE**—State concisely the attainable objectives of the project. Objectives are statements of desired results, not statements of project approach such as collecting data or constructing a model. Relate each objective directly to the problem issue(s). The objectives must be compatible with the problem and approach statements, responsive to cooperator/customer needs, and consistent with the USGS mission. Use caution in setting the objectives and scope to avoid misrepresenting the expected goals of the project.

5. **RELEVANCE and BENEFITS**—Describe the relevance and benefits to the cooperator/customer and the USGS and demonstrate how results will contribute to improved planning and (or) management capabilities and to advancing applied science. Specify the national interest(s) served by the project. A strong Relevance and Benefits section serves to address the Federal interest and mitigate potential conflicts regarding competition with the private sector. Proposed projects should state the relevance of the study to USGS Strategic Science Directions at a minimum; statements of relevance to WMA Strategic Directions, Cooperative Water Program (CWP) priorities (if CWP funds are requested), WSC Science Plans, and (or) other relevant USGS priorities are encouraged. Include any relevant state and local priorities. See **Attachment 2** for guidelines to strengthen this section.

6. **APPROACH**—Describe the tasks, methods, and technologies that constitute the scientific approach proposed to achieve the stated objective(s). A summary describing the science strategy for achieving the objective(s) within the prescribed timeframe and resources should be stated in the first paragraph. The rationale for using the proposed analytical or investigative tools should be explained.

Following the summary description, address the project study plan: a clear logical presentation of the data types, tasks, methods, and sequence of activities for the project. If proven techniques and methods are proposed, then a brief description will suffice. Any unique, innovative, or original method should be described, referenced, and (or) justified. A description of how the data or model output will be analyzed and interpreted to achieve the objective(s) should be included. It is important to describe how results will be evaluated to determine whether the stated objective(s) were achieved.

The approach for complex or research-oriented projects should be organized into subsections that represent phases of the study that show the planned evolution of the study. Sequential numbering of components or a decision flow diagram can be used to show a logical plan for adapting the course of study to the various potential outcomes as the project progresses.

7. **QUALITY ASSURANCE/QUALITY CONTROL**— Describe the QA procedures that will be used to guide data-collection and review activities for the project. For standard data collection, simply cite the Science Center QA Plan or other pertinent documents, such as the National Field Manual, Techniques and Methods reports, or WMA Technical Memoranda.

For all water-quality projects, specify the numbers of each type of QC sample (blanks, replicates, and spikes) that will be collected for each constituent group. If an outside laboratory will be used, indicate that a laboratory evaluation will be made in accordance with Office of Water Quality Technical Memorandum 2007.01. Ensure that the project budget includes adequate time and resources to accomplish the specified QC components. Some projects involving other Federal agencies require preparation, review, and approval of a Quality Assurance Project Plan (QAPP) prior to any environmental data collection. Indicate whether a QAPP will be required, and if so, describe the added time and expense.

8. **PRODUCTS**—Describe the planned information product(s) as well as data types to be produced by the project. Identify any planned publications by series, for example journal article, USGS Scientific Investigations Report, etc. For data projects, also identify the types of data to be produced. A description of USGS report series is available at *http://www.usgs.gov/usgs-manual/1100/1100-3appendixa.pdf.*

9. **REFERENCES**—A list of references cited in the proposal is a beneficial component of the proposed study. Follow accepted USGS style suggestions for formatting citations in the text and the references in this section. Provide links to references with persistent URLs.

10. **TIMELINE**—List major study tasks and major elements of tasks identified in the body of the proposal and indicate starting dates, periods of activity, and ending dates. The timeline is critical to assessing the technical and programmatic feasibility of the project as it provides the basis to evaluate the sequencing of activities and planned duration of the project. A timeline is most often presented in a table or spreadsheet format.

11. **PERSONNEL**—List personnel needs by required skill (QW specialist, technical specialist, hydrogeologist, hydrologic modeler, etc). Identify location of staff (other WSCs, other Mission Areas, other agencies) as well as collaborative work to be accomplished by cooperator staff. Planned contract work should also be described.

12. **BUDGET SUMMARY**—Compile a table of estimated costs for the duration of the project but not to exceed 5 years. The cost estimate in the proposal budget and on the Project Proposal Cover Sheet must agree. Costs can be itemized by task (for example, sampling, laboratory analyses, QA/QC documentation, data analysis, simulation, information product preparation and publication) and (or) by accounting category (for

example, salary, equipment purchases, travel, contracts).

C. Job Hazard Analysis (JHA) for New Projects The JHA should concisely state any safety concerns/elements of the project and the requirements needed to address these safety concerns/elements, such as safety training and equipment needed to allow an employee to perform the work in a safe manner and to ensure that unnecessary liabilities are not incurred by the U.S. Government. All work on hazardous waste sites or work in confined spaces, etc., which would require specialized training and perhaps medical examinations, must be considered when planning the project. A JHA template is located at (*http://water.usgs.gov/usgs/wsft/proposals/JHA-template.pdf*). The JHA must be signed by the Collateral Duty Safety Officer and the Science Center Director. The Regional Safety Officer is responsible for reviewing the proposal JHA. Safety and the requirements to maintain a safe work environment are discussed in a number of Department, Bureau, and Discipline memoranda. A listing of safety memos by category can be found on the web at *http://1stop.usgs.gov/safety/memos/memo-category.shtml*

Attachment 2
STRENGTHENING THE RELEVANCE AND BENEFITS SECTION OF PROPOSALS

It is important that the USGS conduct business that clearly is within our mission, and to the extent possible, does not overtly compete with private entities. Water Mission Area Policy Memorandum No. 2012.01 *http://water.usgs.gov/coop/about/avoiding_competition.pdf* discusses the importance of demonstrating that proposed work is USGS-mission relevant and that it is beneficial to Federal science interests as well as the needs of stakeholders and the public. In this regard, the Water Science Field Team (WSFT) suggests that one way to demonstrate the relevance of our work to the public and the priorities and directions for USGS activities is to include a comprehensive, strong, and supportive Relevance and Benefits section in USGS proposals. By way of example, the following provides some generic statements/areas that should be addressed in the Relevance and Benefits section of proposals.

1. Include benefits that relate to the USGS as a leader in collecting, maintaining, and providing long-term, earth-science data and conducting long-term, broad-scale, multidisciplinary studies that also relate to our investment in core competencies, including fundamental science research. Of necessity, this benefit also relates to our commitment to the Federal Government and the citizens of the United States. For example:

"Completion of the proposed work will provide the USGS with additional water-quality information on multi-reservoirs in mixed land-use settings. These data will add to the USGS national database and will assist in understanding and describing the Nation's water resources."

"The USGS would benefit by keeping current on hydrologic data, analyses, and interpretations of the resources in the X, and from the increased capability of MODFLOW, which would allow it to be applied in a variety of new situations for which integrated modeling tools currently do not exist."

"The USGS would benefit from a better understanding of the mechanics of local scour and the hydraulics of open-channel flow at piers and abutments. The existing national database of about 400 scour measurements would be expanded to include data representing some of the varying physiography in X."

"The study will contribute to the USGS mission by increasing understanding of surface water/

groundwater interactions and their effect on water availability and quality in a common hydrogeologic setting."

2. Include specific benefits that the data collection, results, and interpretations will provide to the customer. For example:
"The results of this study will provide the cooperator with documentation of baseline water quality conditions in the reservoir. This information will help the cooperator to evaluate current and future reservoir management activities with regard to its use as a drinking-water source."

3. Include benefits that might affect other managing parties or agencies involved in hydrologic issues. Stress the high quality of the data and information that will be provided and how it will be used by resource managers. For example:
"The findings of the study will provide managers with reliable and impartial information for their use in reducing property losses associated with damage to homes and cropland in the study area."

4. Include benefits that relate to the importance of our partnerships and exchange of scientific information. For example:
"The cooperator will benefit by having the USGS serve as an unbiased third party with extensive technical expertise on many topics related to X. If the identified approaches herein prove successful, agencies such as USGS, FEMA, USCOE, and others, along with consulting firms, will benefit greatly by having statistically quantifiable, consistent, reproducible, and defensible estimates of peak-flow frequency for regulated streams in X."

5. Include benefits that might relate to the general public or private individuals and companies. For example:
"The public will gain an improved understanding of the source of their water supply."
"The data will be useful to private individuals and companies examining the potential to develop the X aquifers."
The WSFT reviews the Relevance and Benefits section of Science Center proposals with an eye toward attempting to satisfy any inquiries that might arise from our involvement in the study and to ensure that the benefits are appropriately described. References that may prove helpful in writing the Relevance and Benefits section include the USGS Science Strategy (*http://internal.usgs.gov/director/science_strategy/*) and the USGS Water Resources 5-Year Program Plans (*http://water.usgs.gov/usgs/prgmplans/*).

William H. Werkheiser
Associate Director for Water
12201 Sunrise Valley Drive, MS 150
Reston, VA 20192
703-648-4557

March 30, 2010

WATER RESOURCES DIVISION TECHNICAL MEMORANDUM 2010.02

Distribution: GS-W All
  cc: GS-D Regional Executives

From: Matthew C. Larsen
               Associate Director for Water

Subject: WRD Policy Numbered Memorandum No. 2010.02
               Continuous Records Processing of all Water Time Series Data

Because of increasing availability and use of U.S. Geological Survey (USGS) stream gaging, water-quality monitoring, and other time-series hydrologic data in real-time decision making processes, users have requested that data be approved or published much sooner after collection than has been USGS policy in the past. As a result, all Water Science Centers (WSCs) shall implement Continuous Records Processing (CRP) of all water time-series data by **June 30, 2010 with the full understanding that it may take some time for full implementation.** Continuous records processing is the collection, analysis, review, and approval of time-series hydrologic data on a continuous (sub-water year) basis. At any given time, the time-series data will be as close to approval as computational methods and hydrologic interpretation will allow. This general definition of CRP is implemented through the following operational timelines:

1. All real-time water data must be reviewed by a hydrographer and checked for gross instrument errors within 1 day of collection (WRD Policy Memorandum 99.34).
2. All time-series data collected at Category 1 sites (defined below and in attachment 1) are to be finalized within the National Water Information System (NWIS) within 150 days of collection.
3. All time-series data collected at Category 2 sites (defined below and in attachment 1) are to be finalized within NWIS within 240 days of collection.
4. Ultimately, regardless of category, all data need to be approved, finalized, and published (per Water Science Center policy) as part of the Annual Water Data Report by April 1 of the year following the water year of collection.

There are two basic guiding principles implicit in this definition. The first is that CRP must be <u>data driven</u>. This means that streamflow, groundwater levels, water-quality parameters, or other time-series information are not approved until the analyst and reviewers are satisfied that the data are ready for approval and distribution without caveat. The approval criteria will depend on the individual site and its climatic and hydraulic characteristics, the stability of those characteristics, and the field protocols being used at that site. With this principle as a guide, data need to be reviewed and approved as soon as possible after all the necessary information becomes available. Resources must be allocated and prioritized to facilitate this timely review and approval.

The WSCs are to categorize their sites according to the criteria set up in the *Continuous Records Processing Implementation Plan- May 2008* (attachment 1) which was prepared by the Continuous Records Processing Implementation Committee. Because most real-time sites are currently surface-water sites, these categorizations will initially be tracked by the Office of Surface Water with the intention that an official database (NWIS or Station Information Management System (SIMS)) will eventually be used to track the categorization of sites. Category 1 sites are defined as sites for which the data needed to compute records for a period between site visits are in hand at the end of a site visit. These time-series records should be finalized within 150 days of collection. Category 2 sites are defined as sites for which more data are needed for specific seasonal record computation (such as long term ice effect), stream gages that have unstable controls and longer periods are needed to determine trends, or where data from continuous water-quality analyzers depend upon laboratory results for verification. Category 2 time series records should be finalized within 240 days of collection. Category 3 sites are special cases where a continuous record processing does not currently apply. These types of sites should be rare and each case may be unique.

The second guiding principle is that CRP cannot degrade the accuracy of the hydrologic information published by the USGS. High standards of accuracy and precision must be maintained in all data collection and analysis procedures. The USGS must provide the best data to the public as soon as possible.

A number of recommended practices are included in the *Continuous Records Processing Implementation Plan* (attachment 1). WSCs are urged to read the plan and consider adopting those practices that will help meet the goal of full implementation of continuous processing of time series data within the Water Resources Discipline.

Attachment 1 – Continuous Records Processing Implementation Plan – May 2008 (available at *http://water.usgs.gov/admin/memo/policy/wrdpolicy10.02_attachment1.pdf*)

OGW 12.01 Policy for evaluation of well integrity for water-level measurements - initial application to CBR

network wells and test phase for all wells

November 4, 2011

OFFICE OF GROUNDWATER TECHNICAL MEMORANDUM 2012.01

SUBJECT: Policy for evaluation of well integrity for water-level measurements—initial application to CBR network wells and test phase for all wells

Introduction

Water-level measurements play an important role in tracking the status of a groundwater resource. In order to ensure that a water-level measurement adequately represents the hydraulic head in the groundwater system penetrated by the open interval of the well, it is necessary to assure that the well is in good hydraulic connection with the groundwater system and that this connection has not changed over time. Well integrity should be evaluated routinely for USGS groundwater-level observation wells that are part of a recurring measurement program. Well integrity also should be evaluated for wells measured regularly, but less frequently, such as wells in a synoptic or mass measurement program.

The process of evaluating well integrity differs depending on well construction, well access, frequency of measurement, and other factors. Depending on these factors, well integrity may be evaluated by analyzing water-level measurements, by physical tests, or by a combination of these techniques. The process of evaluating well integrity for water-level measurements described in this memo relies heavily on the use of basic hydrologic principles and proper documentation.

Purpose of this Memorandum

This memorandum outlines the requirement that all wells funded under the federal Collection of Basic Records (CBR) Program must undergo a routine evaluation of well integrity. In addition, the Office of Groundwater is considering policy options for evaluating well integrity for all USGS groundwater-level observation wells. USGS observation wells include wells measured by USGS personnel and those wells measured by observers. Other organizations that furnish data to the USGS should have similar methods and procedures as the USGS so as to ensure the data that are being published are from wells that are connected to the aquifer in which they are completed. Centers that publish data (including data served on the Internet) from wells measured by other organizations should encourage the agencies furnishing record to adopt the USGS well-integrity procedures or develop their own procedures. Implementation of the policy for CBR wells will allow Water Science Centers, the Water Science Field Team Groundwater Specialists, and the Office of Groundwater to evaluate the requirement for wider implementation for wells not in the CBR program.

Policy for wells in the CBR network

This policy is presented in terms of office- and field-based procedures. The office-based procedures must be followed for all CBR wells and are recommended for all wells. Implementation of the field-based procedures is more flexible, based on the judgment of the Center Groundwater Specialist.

Office-Based Evaluation of Well Integrity

Annual Hydrograph Check

- Check water-level fluctuations in the well over time and look for indications of a change in well performance, such as a change in the response of the well or a noticeable change in the range of responses. This should be done annually for wells with continuous or frequent measurements. These observations should be documented in the paper site folder, station analysis, or other digital documentation for the well, such as the Site Information Management System (SIMS).

Field-Based Evaluation of Well Integrity

Each Site Visit

- Check the physical condition of the well and well installation and document these observations in the site folder. Changes in and around the well may have an effect on well integrity in the short- or long-term.

Annual Total Depth Measurement

- If access to the well is suitable for a total depth (sounding) measurement, check the depth of the well. If the recorded depth of the well has changed significantly, or the depth indicates that the effective open-screen length has decreased significantly, then well integrity could be compromised and additional testing may be necessary. A method for measuring well depth by use of a graduated steel tape is outlined in USGS Groundwater Procedures Document 11 (Cunningham and Schalk, 2011). The total depth measurement should be documented in the paper site folder, station analysis, or other digital documentation for the well. If access to the well is unsuitable for a total depth measurement, this also should be documented.

Periodic Hydraulic Testing

- If access to the well is suitable for a hydraulic test, some type of repeatable hydraulic test must be conducted upon site establishment, and as necessary throughout the life of the well. As described above, the field evaluation, annual measurement of total depth, and annual evaluation of the hydrograph will provide a good initial check on well integrity. But a quantitative measure of well performance/integrity is valuable and necessary periodically, whenever the above evaluation methods indicate a possible degradation in well performance. The policy for observation well hydraulic testing is summarized in the steps listed below.
    1. Upon establishment of a new well in a measurement program, conduct a baseline hydraulic test (additional detail provided in attachment "Types of Hydraulic Tests for Well Integrity"). Document the results in the site folder or digital documentation for the well. Future tests will be compared to these baseline test results. If a baseline test was not done when the site was established, it should be done as soon as possible.
    2. Conduct the annual hydrograph check, the site visit check for well physical condition, and the annual measurement of total depth as described above.

3.   If the evaluation in step number 2 suggests a degradation of well integrity, repeat the hydraulic test. If the water-level response from the repeat hydraulic test differs significantly from previous tests, the well should be examined more thoroughly (perhaps by using geophysical techniques) and a decision made whether to rehabilitate the well (such as by redeveloping) or to properly abandon the well.

4.   The evaluations described in step number 2 above may not always detect degraded well integrity. Thus a hydraulic test should be repeated as time and resources permit, and re-testing is recommended every 3–5 years for all wells in critical networks or used in critical management decisions. The term "critical" is subjective but should include monitoring wells that a cooperator or the public uses to evaluate the effects of nearby groundwater depletions, climate change, or groundwater/surface-water interaction.

5.   Each step of the well integrity evaluation must be documented in the paper site folder, station analysis, or other digital documentation for the well

Evaluation for wells not in the CBR network

The above policy will immediately apply to CBR network wells and its application will be evaluated for wells not in the CBR network based on input from Water Science Center and WSFT Groundwater Specialists. The Centers are encouraged to apply the policy to all wells, regardless of whether they are in the CBR network, in order to appropriately evaluate the policy. There are some special cases where implementation of the policy is not feasible or burdensome and the Office of Groundwater would like to identify these
cases in order to determine appropriate approaches for evaluating well integrity. One such case is for wells measured infrequently (less than once per year or part of synoptic measurements).

Prospective Evaluation Approach for Wells Measured Less Frequently Than Once per Year

Some network wells are measured infrequently, but are in a regular measurement program. This is common for wells that are part of a synoptic or mass measurement program. Potentiometric surface maps commonly are produced from these measurements. Even though these wells are measured infrequently, it is important that their integrity be evaluated.

Each measurement should be evaluated by comparing it to past measurements. If a measurement is outside the range of expected measurements, as suggested from past measurements, it should be re-evaluated. If potentiometric surface maps are made from the water-level measurements, any measurement that seems to deviate from the conceptual model of the groundwater-flow system should be re-evaluated. Best hydrologic judgment should be used to determine the accuracy of the measurement and the extent to which the measured value is representative of the aquifer hydraulic head. If measurements are judged to be anomalous, field-related well integrity checks may be needed to determine the integrity of the well; methods such as total well depth measurement (and comparison to previous depth measurements), well-integrity hydraulic tests, borehole geophysical logs, and borehole camera surveys can be used for this purpose.

Water Science Center Performance Evaluation

The Water Science Field Team Groundwater Specialists and the Office of Groundwater representatives will review the well-integrity documentation during the triennial Water Science Center Technical

Reviews. In addition, the Water Science Field Team Groundwater Specialists and the Office of Groundwater encourages Water Science Center personnel to develop effective screening tools to evaluate well integrity for wells with continuous measurements and to share these with the groundwater community.

References cited

Cunningham, W.L., and Schalk, C.W., comps., 2011, GWPD 11-Measuring well depth by use of a graduated steel tape (Version: 2010.1): in Groundwater technical procedures of the U.S. Geological Survey (Cunningham, W. L., and Schalk, C.W., comps.): U.S. Geological Survey Techniques and Methods 1–A1, 151 p. (available only online at *http://pubs.usgs.gov/tm/1a1/*).

Cunningham, W.L., and Schalk, C.W., comps., 2011, GWPD 17-Conducting an instantaneous change in head (Slug) test with a mechanical slug and a submersible pressure transducer (Version: 2010.1): in Groundwater technical procedures of the U.S. Geological Survey (Cunningham, W. L., and Schalk, C.W., comps.): U.S. Geological Survey Techniques and Methods 1–A1, 151 p. (available only online at *http://pubs.usgs.gov/tm/1a1/*).

William M. Alley /s/
Chief, Office of Groundwater

Distribution (bcc): GS-W WSC Directors, GS-W CD, GS-W A, GS-W GW All, OGW

ATTACHMENT: Types of Hydraulic Tests for Well Integrity

ATTACHMENT

Types of Hydraulic Tests for Well Integrity

A change in hydraulic test results over time is an indicator of a change in well integrity. The approach used for a hydraulic test is to induce a change in water level in the well and measure the water level as it returns to equilibrium. This test can be done in many ways, and some flexibility is necessary based on well construction, well accessibility, and instrument configuration, for example.

A single-well "slug test" using a mechanical slug or air (pneumatic test) is recommended for wells in a regular measurement program such as the Collection of Basic Records (CBR) Program. If a single-well test using a mechanical slug or air is not possible, another repeatable approach to induce water-level change in the well must be used. This can be done using a pump, bailer, or by pouring clean water into the well. Method repeatability over time is a key aspect to the choice of method. All future tests should be run identically to the baseline test in order to simplify the comparison of results. The text below provides basic guidance on several types of tests. Details for each type are available in the literature (for example, Butler, 1998).

Mechanical slug

USGS field procedures for conducting a mechanical slug test are provided in Groundwater Technical Procedure 17 (Cunningham and Schalk, 2011).

Pneumatic slug

A pneumatic slug test differs from a mechanical slug test in that the initiation of the change in water level is accomplished with air pressure. This test requires the ability to seal the top of the well and pressurize the well, which lowers the water level; then, the sudden release of the pressure results in the rise of water level. Such tests are always conducted using a pressure transducer, data logger, and field computer. If pressurization is instantaneous, both a falling-head and rising-head test can be conducted. Most of the time, however, well pressurization is not instantaneous and only the rising-head part of the test can be evaluated.

Poured slug

A poured slug test initiates the water-level change by pouring a known volume of water into the well. Use of deionized water is preferable. However, if an observation well is being tested, and no water-quality samples are collected, use of tap water may be acceptable. Because this test creates a sudden rise in the water level, only a falling head test can be conducted. An electric tape, steel tape, or pressure transducer and data logger can be used to record the water level as the water level returns to the pre-test (static) conditions.

Bailing the well

A bailer test initiates the water-level change by suddenly removing a known volume of water from the well using a bailer. The bailer is lowered into the well and allowed to fill with water; rapid removal of the filled bailer creates a sudden drop in water level. The subsequent water-level rise, and return to the static water level, is measured over time. Thus, only a rising head test can be conducted. An electric tape, steel tape, or pressure transducer and data logger can be used to record the water level as the water level returns to the pre-test (static) water level.

Pumping the well

Well tests that involve the pumping of a well (for example, a specific capacity test) are usually not required because of the additional time and equipment required. The USGS measures many irrigation, production, and public water supply wells. Some of these wells have dedicated pumps and some do not. Wells that are pumped regularly, probably are in good connection with the aquifer and do not have to be tested unless there is some indication of decreasing connection. The Water Science Centers, however, may want to take advantage of wells that have a pump installed but are not regularly pumped. These might be back up wells in a public water supply well field, or back up irrigation wells that are used only when surface water is not available. Slug tests may not be effective for wells like this, so using the dedicated pump to determine specific capacity might be the Water Science Center's most feasible option to check well integrity. A baseline specific capacity test (run by the USGS or reported from the original well installation) would be helpful in cases of suspected anomalous water-level measurements.

Key points for all methods

The purpose of the hydraulic test for well integrity is to determine if the response of the well has changed over time. The goal is not to calculate aquifer properties, although it might be a useful additional step. Regardless of the method used to induce water-level change, the following points are relevant for a well-integrity test:

- Document the volume of the slug and calculate the maximum water-level change in the site folder or digital documentation for the well. You should attempt to match this water-level change during any future tests. If the hydraulic test approach is the same among tests, a change in well integrity can be evaluated directly based on the change in water-level recovery time.
- The initial rising or falling head test may be terminated when (a) the water level is equal to the initial water level, or (b) readings change less than 0.01 ft per 10 minutes, or (c) thirty minutes have elapsed.
- If a mechanical slug-test is performed, a second test can be conducted upon removal of the slug if the water level has returned to the initial water level within 30 minutes.
- Document the time it took the water levels to return to the initial water level for all tests. If the water levels in the well did not return to initial levels within 30 minutes, document the percent recovery that occurred in 30 minutes.

- With some additional parameters, an analysis of hydraulic conductivity is possible using all of these methods. However, analysis for hydraulic conductivity is not required by this policy.

In summary, the main objective of a well-integrity test is to evaluate the hydraulic connection between the well and the aquifer. The Water Science Center staff has flexibility to determine the best method to accomplish this objective. An important aspect is reproducibility, so that, future tests can be compared to tests already conducted and documented.

References

Butler, J.J., Jr., 1998, The design, performance, and analysis of slug tests: Lewis Publishers, Boca Raton, FL, 252 p.

Cunningham, W.L., and Schalk, C.W., comps., 2011, GWPD 17-Conducting an instantaneous change in head (Slug) test with a mechanical slug and a submersible pressure transducer (Version: 2010.1): *in* Groundwater technical procedures of the U.S. Geological Survey (Cunningham, W. L., and Schalk, C.W., comps.): U.S. Geological Survey Techniques and Methods 1–A1, 151 p. (Available online at *http://pubs.usgs.gov/tm/1a1/*)

OGW 11.02 Recommended groundwater field procedures for the U.S. Geological Survey

April 28, 2011

OFFICE OF GROUNDWATER TECHNICAL MEMORANDUM 2011.02

SUBJECT: Recommended groundwater field procedures for the U.S. Geological Survey

The Office of Groundwater is pleased to announce the release of the Techniques and Methods Report Book 1, Chapter A1, "Groundwater technical procedures of the U.S. Geological Survey," compiled by William L. Cunningham and Charles W. Schalk. This is an on-line only report available at: *http://pubs.usgs.gov/tm/1a1/*.

These groundwater technical procedures (GWPDs), which were compiled in 1995 as an internal tool for USGS technicians and hydrologists, have been collected from common techniques cited in USGS reports, USGS internal memoranda, and USGS training programs for many years. Because of the external demand for documentation of these procedures, and the desire to cite them outside of the USGS, they have been reviewed, edited, and compiled in this new report.

These GWPDs are the groundwater field procedures recommended by the Office of Groundwater. They are written in concise language with step-by-step instructions of sufficient detail so that someone with limited experience with the procedure but with a basic understanding of the measurements and general field work can successfully reproduce the procedure unsupervised. The GWPDs do not provide every detail of an individual field task, as the user is expected to have at least nominal field experience. USGS Science Centers may modify them for their circumstances, hydrologic conditions, project objectives, and Center needs. Modifications to these procedures must be documented in the Science Center or project-specific groundwater quality-assurance plan.

The Office of Groundwater recommends downloading the entire document. The Introduction section contains important descriptive information. The electronic report is conveniently hyperlinked to the individual GWPDs from the table of contents or through the Adobe bookmark option on the left hand side of the page. The individual GWPDs also can be downloaded, or referenced by use of the persistent URL. GWPDs will be updated periodically as errors are detected or new standard techniques evolve. Each procedure is consecutively numbered and contains a version number/date. Any citation of an individual procedure should include the version number of the procedure as an integral part of the reference. New procedures will be made available as they are developed, and general electronic announcements will accompany releases of new GWPDs.

OGW recognizes that there may be a need to access superseded versions of the GWPDs for historical reference. An archive of superseded GWPDs will be maintained on the Office of Groundwater web site at *http://water.usgs.gov/ogw/GWPD/*. This online archive will provide all users with access to the most current version of the GWPDs, any superseded GWPDs from TM1-A1. Internal USGS users will have access to the superseded original internal GWPDs from 1995 and 2008.

Comments or suggestions about the subject report should be addressed to Bill Cunningham in the Office of Groundwater, 703-648-5005 or *wcunning@usgs.gov*.

William M. Alley
Chief, Office of Groundwater

OGW 11.01 PROGRAMS AND PLANS—Groundwater Flow and Transport Model Archival

February 7, 2011

OFFICE OF GROUNDWATER TECHNICAL MEMORANDUM 2011.01

SUBJECT: PROGRAMS AND PLANS—Groundwater Flow and Transport Model Archival

Groundwater models are often an integral part of U.S. Geological Survey (USGS) investigations and the conclusions published in USGS reports often are based on results of these models. As a result, several Office of Groundwater (OGW) policy memorandums have given guidance and requirements for documentation and archival of groundwater flow and transport models. We list four of these memorandums at the end of this memo. The primary purpose of this memorandum is to update the policy for model archival.

All groundwater flow and transport models that are a significant part of groundwater investigations must be archived as specified in Office of Groundwater (OGW) Technical Memorandum 00.02 (*http://water.usgs.gov/admin/memo/GW/gw00.02.html*). The Water Science Field Team (WSFT) Groundwater Specialists act on behalf of the Office of Groundwater to assure that all required information is present in the archive and to verify compliance with the policy. This policy continues as before with two additions effective for models with completion dates of March 2011 or later.

One addition to the policy is that the general boundaries of the model (the latitude and longitude of the corners of a rectangle outlining the model grid area) should be included in a text file (filename: modelgeoref.txt) that contains the georeferencing information and is filed at the upper level directory of that particular model archive. This will document the area under study and allow for future map displays of the availability of models developed by the USGS.

The second addition to the policy is that all reports that contain groundwater flow and transport models must have their model archive reviewed and approved by the WSFT Groundwater Specialist before the report is submitted to the Bureau Approving Official for approval. This requirement has been in place in the former Northeast and Southeast Regions for some years and is now extended nationwide, as discussed further below.

There has been increased interest in obtaining models from the model archives by public and private entities. Many of our cooperators run our archived models. With greater use, it is increasingly important that the archives exist and can duplicate information in our published reports. Technical reviews of the Water Science Centers (WSC) have found model archives sometimes are insufficient to duplicate the model results, there is a significant delay in creating the archives, or archives are never completed.

Prior to submission of a groundwater modeling report to the Bureau Approving Official, the WSC Director or their designee (typically the WSC Groundwater Specialist) should review the archive to ensure compliance with OGW Technical Memorandum 00.02. The archived model needs to be run and the output compared with the text, figures, and tables in the report to ensure that the data are comparable. The WSC should then notify the WSFT Groundwater Specialist that the report and archive are available for review. The archive, report, and associated technical reviews should be transmitted to the WSFT Groundwater Specialist who will verify proper archival and ensure compliance with other OGW technical memorandums. The WSFT Groundwater Specialist will notify the originating Center by memorandum whether the archive complies with OGW requirements. After any issues are addressed, the report and associated materials, including documentation of the WSFT Groundwater Specialist review and approval of the archive, can be transmitted to the Bureau Approving Official for final approval.

Memorandums on groundwater flow and transport models:

- OGW Technical memorandum 96.04--PUBLICATIONS--Policy on documenting the use of groundwater simulation in project reports (*http://water.usgs.gov/admin/memo/GW/gw96.04.html*)
- OGW Technical memorandum 97.01--Clarification of policy for using non-USGS computer programs in groundwater projects (*http://water.usgs.gov/admin/memo/GW/gw97.01.html*)
- OGW Technical Memorandum 00.02--PROGRAMS AND PLANS--Update of the National Policy to Archive Ground Water Flow and Transport Models (*http://water.usgs.gov/admin/memo/GW/gw00.02.html*)
- OGW Technical memorandum 2005.02--PUBLICATIONS--Policy on documenting the results of new simulations using previously published groundwater models (*http://water.usgs.gov/admin/memo/GW/gw05.02.html*)

William M. Alley
Chief, Office of Groundwater

OGW 10.01 Update of the National Policy to Archive Borehole-Geophysical Logs

October 13, 2009

Office of Groundwater Technical Memorandum 2010.01

Subject: PROGRAMS AND PLANS — Update of the National Policy to Archive Borehole-Geophysical Logs

In 2000, a national policy to archive borehole-geophysical logs was established by OGW Technical Memorandum 00.03. Since that time, the Log ASCII Standard (*http://cwls.org/las_info.php*) has become the accepted format for storage and transmittal of log data in the geophysical and groundwater science community. All widely used software for geophysical log collection and analysis now automatically generates and reads LAS-formatted data. Although the present archive policy allows for archive of log data in other ASCII formats, the current situation strongly indicates that LAS should become the standard format for log archival within the USGS. This memorandum updates OGW Technical Memorandum 00.03 and establishes a new requirement that geophysical logs be archived on the USGS Water Science Center's computer database in LAS format. This memorandum clarifies archiving of image-log data, log-type codes, corrections/shifts/post processing, log annotations, and NWIS Logs records. This memorandum introduces a web-based system to be used for the proper archiving of log data files and headers.

LAS Formatted Logs:
Borehole-geophysical logs are to be archived in LAS 2.0 unwrapped format as one the following groups of log types:

1. Individual log of a single parameter collected with a single probe (such as a caliper log);
2. Combination log of multiple depth-adjusted parameters collected with a single probe (such as a multi-function electric log); or
3. Composite logs of multiple depth-adjusted parameters collected with multiple probes that have been depth corrected.

As policy, an NWIS site must be established for each logged borehole. Geophysical logs should be archived by the Water Science Centers on a locally-based computer system under a main directory called LOGARCHIVE. Subdirectories for each NWIS 15-digit Site ID number, as previously required, are no longer needed. Each geophysical log file name will include the NWIS 15-digit Site ID number, date of log collection (year month day), two-letter log-type code, and a sequence number. In addition, the file name will include the ".LAS" extension to indicate it is archived in LAS format. The first log of the same type collected on a particular day would have a sequence number of 01, the second, 02, etc. An example path name for an archived log would be:

LOGARCHIVE>424531077564201.20000601.MI01.LAS

Image-Log Data:
Image-log data from acoustic- and optical-televiewers are not conducive for conversion to the LAS format, so they should be archived in their original binary format and if desired in commonly used

image formats such as jpeg, tiff, or PDF. An executable file of any software needed for analysis of original binary formatted geophysical log files should be included in the LOGARCHIVE with explanation of security measures for proprietary programs. Files archived in an original binary format should be archived with the same naming convention as a LAS file except that it will include the file extension assigned by the software manufacturer (.log or .rd for example). The file naming convention for extracted images (jpeg, tiff) and PDFs will use a zero date, must be sequentially numbered (IMG01 … IMG02, PDF01 … PDF02) and include the proper extension depending on the type of file archived. Examples of archived files would be:

LOGARCHIVE>424531077564201.20000601.AT01.log (acoustic televiewer archived as an original binary file)
LOGARCHIVE>424531077564201.00000000.PDF01.pdf (the first PDF file archived for this site)
LOGARCHIVE>424531077564201.00000000.IMG01.jpg (the first image file archived for this site)

Log-Type Codes:
The master list of geophysical log-type codes is available from the OGW internal web page (*http://water.usgs.gov/usgs/ogw/bgas/borehole_archiving/*). All efforts should be made to properly categorize the log into one of these existing log types. Requests for additional log types should be directed to the OGW Borehole Geophysics Advisor (*jhwillia@usgs.gov*).

Corrections/Shifts/Post Processing
Borehole-geophysical logs archived in the Water Science Center's database should be the final corrected version of the logs. All corrections, depth shifts, and post processing must be complete to assure the log is referenced to the designated measuring point and that the data are complete and accurate. If necessary, any notes on post processing can be included in the remarks field of the log header.

Log Annotations
The condition of the borehole (mud- or water-filled for example) and size of the hole at the time of logging should be noted in the remarks or hydrologic conditions section of the log header. This information is critical for log analysis and interpretation. In addition, any conditions that influence depth-specific log data should be noted along with the depth of the occurrence. For example, if a caliper tool sticks and the diameter readings are influenced, then a notation for that depth should be made. If numerous depth-specific annotations are required, then a posting text file can be archived along with the borehole logs to provide additional information. New software has been developed for log annotations.

NWIS Logs Records
A log record must be entered into NWIS for each borehole-geophysical log archived in the Water Science Center's database. These records are not automatically added but are necessary to assure conformity with NWIS architecture. New software has been developed for generating the logs records.

Web-Based Archiving System:
A new USGS web-based system has been developed for archiving LAS files as well as addressing many of the issues described in this memorandum. Users can access the system from the following URL: *http://logarchiver.usgs.gov*. The web-based system should be used to archive newly collected geophysical logs and to transfer existing logs archived in each Centers' computer database to the

approved format. Through the application of the web-based system and associated software, the OGW will assist each Center in the transfer of their geophysical logs that have been previously archived following the guidelines presented in OGW Technical Memorandum 00.03.

Header templates for the widely used WellCAD log-analysis software are available from the OGW internal web page (*http://water.usgs.gov/usgs/ogw/bgas/borehole_archiving/*). The templates are interfaced with the new USGS web-based system to generate LAS-compatible headers for individual, combination, and composite log archives in English or metric units.

The Regional Groundwater Specialists are to act on behalf of the Office of Groundwater to assure that the borehole-geophysical logs collected by the Water Science Centers are properly archived.

Adherence to the updated policy of archiving borehole-geophysical logs will ensure that data collected by the USGS Water Science Centers will remain available in a readily usable format for support of published reports, future scientific investigations, and data requests from the public.

William M. Alley
Chief, Office of Groundwater

OGW 09.02 Establishment of a National Policy to Archive Surface-Geophysical Data

February 5, 2009

OFFICE OF GROUND WATER TECHNICAL MEMORANDUM 2009.02

SUBJECT: Establishment of a National Policy to Archive Surface-Geophysical Data

The U. S. Geological Survey (USGS) collects surface-geophysical data as part of many water-resource investigations. At present, there is no standardized format for storing digital surface-geophysical data and there is no readily available means to store the data in the National Water Information System (NWIS). The purpose of this memorandum is to provide policy and guidance for archiving surface-geophysical data to preserve them for future review and use.

This surface-geophysical data archive policy is in accordance with USGS policy that states that all field notes, measurements, and observations shall be archived indefinitely (Hubbard, 1992). The fundamental purpose of the archive is to store original data, record the unique details of the data collection, and document the hydrologic conditions under which the data were collected. Through this archive policy, surface-geophysical data and metadata will be readily accessible for future research, analyses, reinterpretation, and reproducibility testing. Each USGS Water Science Center (WSC) collecting surface-geophysical data must have a written policy for data management and permanent file archiving procedures. This policy should be documented in the Center's Data-Management Plan and Archiving Plan, both of which are a necessary part of the Center's overall Ground-Water Quality Assurance Plan (see Brunett and others, 1997 for details). The Archive Plan must be consistent with WRD's scientific records management policy and applicable records disposition schedules (*http://water.usgs.gov/usgs/srm/*).

As more surface-geophysical data collection methods become digital, the ability to archive data is facilitated. Any electronic files created with a surface-geophysical survey must be permanently archived along with all paper field notes. Field notes should document the date and time of field collection, along with the names of all electronic files. Paper copies of maps, sketches, and raw data should be electronically scanned and saved. When possible, proprietary binary files should be exported to ASCII format. All data that cannot be converted to ASCII format should be archived in the original binary format along with versions of the software used for viewing, processing, and (or) displaying the data. In addition, data that are displayed in profiles or plots should be stored in graphic file or printable-document format (pdf). Although most data are digital, some analog data are still collected. This archive policy requires that analog data be "digitized" by typing results into a digital file and archived for future use. Examples of analog data include manually recorded instrument readings, such as (but not limited to) data from electromagnetic induction or gravity meters. If it is infeasible to digitize the results, the analog charts or recorded information should be archived as paper files or pdf files.

Information critical to each data set should be preserved along with the raw data. Mandatory elements for archiving surface-geophysical data are listed in table 1 and are compatible with NWIS header information. Elements critical to specific surface-geophysical methods are listed in table 2. Because new surface-geophysical methods and equipment are continually being developed, the list of equipment in table 2 is not exhaustive and should be considered a guideline for each Center's Ground Water Quality

Assurance Plan, which includes a surface-geophysical archive plan. The surface-geophysical archive plan should detail the following critical elements:

- Handling, back-up, and storage procedures for electronic data at time of data collection. It is recommended that, at a minimum, all digital data be temporarily backed up on a removable, non-volatile data storage medium (e.g. CD-ROM, flash drive, etc.) or permanently stored on a server at the end of each day.
- A list of all surface-geophysical methods used by the Center and codes for naming conventions
- A specific database structure including: server, main directory (called SG-Archive), sub-directories, and file naming structure. Each directory should include a "readme" file that describes the contents of the directory, references to any publications that include the data and (or) analyses of the data, and information on software used to acquire or interpret the data. The "readme" file should be in plain ASCII text format. Examples of database structures are given at *http://water.usgs.gov/usgs/ogw/bgas/surface_archiving/Data_Structures.pdf*.
- File naming conventions that indicate at a minimum the type of data using the appropriate code (table 2) and a sequence number. In addition, file names can include date, time, profile directions, and (or) location tags.
- Timeframe for when data are archived after data collection.
- Policy for archiving software used to collect, process, and analyze data.
- Policy for back-up procedures for archived data. The electronic archive must be on a computer that is routinely backed up as done for other mission critical information.

Table 1: Summarizes the mandatory elements that should be archived with surface-geophysical data in an ASCII text file (*http://water.usgs.gov/usgs/ogw/bgas/surface_archiving/Table1.pdf*).

Table 2: Summarizes the specific information that should be archived for representative surface-geophysical equipment (*http://water.usgs.gov/usgs/ogw/bgas/surface_archiving/Table2.pdf*).

The Regional Ground-Water Specialists are to act on behalf of the Office of Ground Water (OGW) to review the surface-geophysical data archives of the Water Science Centers during technical reviews. Adherence to systematic backup and archive procedures for surface-geophysical data is a responsibility of Water Science Center staff and management. Proper archiving of the data will ensure data will be available for support of published reports, future scientific investigations, and data requests from the public.

If you have any questions or comments about the policies and guidance in this memo, please contact John W. Lane, Chief, OGW Branch of Geophysics, at *jwlane@usgs.gov*. Additional information, including an editable spreadsheet of mandatory elements, is at *http://water.usgs.gov/usgs/ogw/bgas/surface_archiving/*.

References cited

Brunett, J.O., Barber, N.L, Burns, A.W., Fogelman, R.P., Gilles, D.C., Lidwin, R.A, and Mack, T.J., 1997, A quality-assurance plan for District ground-water activities of the U. S. Geological Survey: U. S. Geological Survey Open-File Report 97-11, 44 p.

Hubbard, E.F., 1992, Policy recommendations for management and retention of hydrologic data of the U. S. Geological Survey: U. S. Geological Survey Open-File Report 92-56, 32 p.

William M. Alley /s/
Chief, Office of Ground Water

OGW 09.01 Update on Guidance for the Preparation, Approval, and Archiving of Aquifer-Test Results

January 7, 2009

OFFICE OF GROUND WATER TECHNICAL MEMORANDUM 2009.01

Subject: Update on Guidance for the Preparation, Approval, and Archiving of Aquifer-Test Results

Analyses of aquifer tests to define the hydraulic characteristics of a specific aquifer or aquifer system are an integral part of our interpretive ground-water investigations. The results of these analyses are critical components of flow-system or solute-transport analyses and important to conclusions published in U.S. Geological Survey (USGS) reports. Consequently, reported aquifer characteristics such as hydraulic conductivity, transmissivity, storativity, and other hydraulic characteristics derived from aquifer-test analyses must be clearly documented and technically defensible. The purpose of this memorandum is to reiterate guidelines and procedures necessary to obtain approval for the results of aquifer tests and to provide guidelines for archival of the test results. This memorandum is an update of Office of Ground Water Technical Memorandum 94.02.

BACKGROUND

According to WRD Publications Guide (U.S. Geological Survey Open-File Report 87-0205, Article 11.01.2) "....calculated hydraulic characteristics such as transmissivity, hydraulic conductivity, and storage coefficient, are interpretive and must be approved by the Director, unless cited from a Director-approved report." Approval of aquifer tests is currently delegated to the Regional Ground-Water Specialists. Approval is required for all calculations of aquifer hydraulic characteristics to be released to the general public, to cooperators, or published in or otherwise used to support the results of investigations reported in USGS-approved reports.

Estimates of aquifer hydraulic characteristics commonly are obtained from "textbook" or published values for various lithologies. These are not considered calculations of aquifer characteristics and do not require approval under the terms of this memorandum. In addition, estimates of transmissivity determined on the basis of specific-capacity measurements do not require approval. Results from well-performance tests (typically slug tests) that are used to check the connection of observation wells with the aquifer also do not require approval, unless they are used to report on aquifer characteristics.

DOCUMENTATION, APPROVAL, AND ARCHIVAL OF AQUIFER-TEST RESULTS

While the USGS encourages the publication of aquifer-test results in reports, it is not feasible to publish the data and graphical results for every test conducted. In all cases, either as part of a formal report or as a separate packet (for archival), aquifer-test results should be submitted to the Regional Ground-Water Specialist for review and subsequent approval. The Regional Ground-Water Specialist reviews the report or aquifer-test packet to assess (1) that the report or packet contains the necessary data and related information to properly analyze the subject test(s), and (2) that the analyses and results are technically defensible.

Elements that typically should be submitted for review are listed below. These elements assume an aquifer test that is comprised of a pumping well and one or more observation wells and should be modified as appropriate for other types of tests such as a single-well slug test. The eight elements are as follows:

1. A brief description of the test which includes the purpose, date, test procedures, and methods of analysis of the results. Any unique or unusual features or problems related to the test or to the collection and analysis of test data should be described. A brief description of the assumptions used in analyzing the test results also should be included, as needed to clarify the test.
2. A sketch of the test site showing the distances from the pumped well to all observation wells and the location of any boundaries, streams, springs, ditches, pumping or flowing wells, or other features that possibly could influence test results. Where the test includes multiple wells, the sketch of the test site should be drawn to scale.
3. Description of test and observation well construction, including screened and open interval(s), casing and screen diameters, and location of filter pack and grouted intervals.
4. A description of the site hydrogeologic characteristics, including sections that show the major water-bearing and confining units. The intervals of the pumping and observation wells that are screened or open should be depicted on the logs or sections.
5. Complete time-discharge records of the pumped well.
6. Complete water-level records and hydrographs showing pre-test trends and water levels during the pumping and recovery phases.
7. Description of methods and computations showing adjustments to drawdown for pre-test trends, adjustments of recovery for projected drawdown, or adjustments to account for extraneous effects not related to pumping or recovery, such as barometric and tidal effects or other interferences.
8. All plots of observed or adjusted drawdown or recovery data used to determine hydraulic characteristics, showing match points (when used) and computations.

It is recognized that in some cases it is not possible to provide a complete description of these eight elements. Investigators are encouraged to discuss their plans with the Regional Ground-Water Specialist to determine the requirements for a particular test packet or report before submitting it for review and approval.

A transmittal memorandum, indicating that the test results have been reviewed by the Science Center Ground-Water Specialist or their designee, shall be included with the aquifer-test packet or report. This review should include some checking of the field data and a verification that the test results are appropriate, given the site hydrogeology, well construction, and test conditions and that the test results have been reviewed independently before being submitted for regional review and approval.

Following approval by the Regional Ground-Water Specialist, the packet or report will be returned to the originating Science Center or office where the hydraulic characteristics and related site and well data should be entered into the National Water Information System (NWIS) and the packet and associated information appropriately archived in a Science Center "aquifer-test archive." These archived aquifer-test files should include the approved aquifer-test packet and the packet-review transmittal memoranda. The aquifer-test archive will be reviewed as a routine part of Science Center ground-water technical reviews.

If computer software is used in the aquifer-test analysis, the policy outlined in Office of Ground Water (OGW) Technical Memorandum 91.04 and clarified in OGW Technical Memorandum 97.01 must be followed. This policy requires that the theoretical basis of the software be documented and that it be demonstrated that a test-data set can be correctly analyzed using the software. Submittal of a computer-software analysis does not eliminate the need for the information described in element 8, above.

The aquifer-test archive can be a paper or electronic archive (or usually a combination of both). Most current aquifer tests will have electronic data collected as a part of conducting the aquifer test (for example, output from a pressure transducer or data logger). These electronic data must be archived. The Science Center has the option of archiving these data in the ADAPS (Automated Data Processing System) subsystem of NWIS or in a local on-line electronic archive subject to the Science Center's regular computer backups. If both a paper and an electronic archive exist, there should be a cross reference indicating the existence of each. That is, the electronic archive should include a "read-me" file explaining where the paper archive is physically located, and the paper archive should include a notation describing the location of the electronic archive.

In the electronic aquifer-test archive, a sub-directory should be created for each aquifer test (or project) and named according to the associated project report (for example, SIR2007-2083 Cedar Rapids) or site location (if the results are not included in a project report). All output from the data-collection equipment should be included in this archive system (for example, data logger output files, output files from data-analysis programs such as AQTESOLV, and summary data files created in other software packages such as Excel). If possible, all files should be saved as text files (ASCII), in addition to any proprietary formats, to ensure that they remain available even if proprietary software changes.

This memorandum discusses documentation, approval, and archival procedures in the context of single- or multiple-well aquifer tests. Aquifer characteristics also may be calculated by other methods, such as, determination of aquifer diffusivity from attenuation of a tidal pulse or flood wave through an aquifer, or using hydrograph-recession characteristics. The same procedures should be followed for these types of analyses, and information in the report or packet must adequately enable reviewers to visualize the physical system, evaluate all data, verify all calculations, and assess that the methods and results are defensible.

In summary, reported aquifer characteristics that are calculated from aquifer tests must be clearly documented and technically defensible. As such, it is required that: (1) the author prepares a formal report or aquifer-test packet that includes the eight elements outlined in this memo; (2) the report/packet is submitted to the Science Center Ground-Water Specialist (or their designee) for technical review of aquifer test analyses; (3) the Science Center Ground-Water Specialist (or their designee) prepares a formal memo of review; (4) the author addresses the Science Center Specialist's comments and transmits the report/packet to the Regional Ground-Water Specialist for aquifer-test review and approval; and (5) once approved, aquifer test results must be archived and entered into NWIS.

William M. Alley /signed/
Chief, Office of Ground Water

This memorandum supersedes Office of Ground Water Technical
Memorandum No. 94.02

March 09, 2006

OFFICE OF GROUND WATER TECHNICAL MEMORANDUM No. 2006.02

SUBJECT: Policy and Archive Guidance for Ground-Water Data Collection using Handheld Computers

The purpose of this memorandum is to provide policy and guidance for ground-water data collection and archive using MONKES software. The memo contains the following information:

1. Background on the MONKES suite of handheld computer programs
2. Recommendations for use of the MONKES1 program
3. Installation, documentation, and support of the MONKES1 program
4. Guidelines for protecting and archiving electronic data from the MONKES1 program

Background on MONKES

The Multi Optional Network Key Entry System (MONKES) is a series of programs on handheld computers for ground-water data entry and processing. MONKES modules were originally created by Steve Predmore (CA), Burl Goree (LA), and Ron Seanor (LA). It is designed to operate on a handheld computer that has a Windows CE Operating System.

The MONKES1 program is used to input and process ground-water level measurements in the field. A new version of MONKES1 (version 3.1) has been expanded to include the collection of site-visit information at wells instrumented with digital recorders. MONKES1 currently is used in more than 18 Water Science Centers. The MONKES2 program is used to enter site data for new ground-water sites and update existing site information. The MONKES3 program is used to enter ground-water water-level and water-quality field data. MONKES2 and MONKES3 currently are available as beta versions.

Recommendations for use of MONKES1

It is the vision of the Office of Ground Water to utilize mobile technology to improve workflow processes in the collection, processing, and quality assurance of our ground-water data. As such, the Office of Ground Water recommends the use of MONKES1 for routine ground-water level data collection throughout the U.S. Geological Survey Water Science Centers. The MONKES1 program offers the following advantages to paper notes:
(1) one time data entry, avoiding transcription and math errors,
(2) immediate data validation against current NWIS reference lists,
(3) easily accessible NWIS site information to verify location of wells,
(4) a listing of latest water-level measurements for data verification,
(5) an immediate check for completeness of record, avoiding inadvertent omission of required fields,
(6) timely data entry into NWIS by use of GWSI batch entry, and
(7) the archive of all site visit data in an XML file which can be easily transferred to a permanent online archive.

Installation, Documentation, and Support of MONKES1

Jerry Feese, Kansas Water Science Center, provides on-going support for MONKES1. For help, email should be sent to the Lotus group GS-W Help MONKES. There is also a MONKES Interest Group, a forum for users of the programs. Email can be sent to this group at GS-W MONKES. Limited support also is provided for MONKES2 and MONKES3, as development of these programs continues.

MONKES1, v3.1 requires a Personal Data Assistant (PDA) handheld computer that has a Windows CE Operating System of Pocket PC 2000, 2002, 2003, or 2003 second edition. MONKES1 has been successfully tested on several models of Pocket PCs. The MONKES programs are not compatible with PDAs using operating systems other than Windows CE, which include Palm, Symbian, Linux, Delphi, and BlackBerry. MONKES 3.1 currently is not compatible with Windows Mobile 5.0 (Pocket PC 2005). However, version 3.1 is currently being ported to .NET, which is compatible with Pocket PC 2005 and is backward compatible with previous versions of Pocket PC. Contact GS-W Help MONKES for an updated list of Pocket PCs that work with MONKES.

MONKES1, v 3.1 is now available. All of the information needed for downloading, installing, and operating the MONKES1 program is available at URL *http://wwwrustla.er.usgs.gov/MONKES1* (this link no longer active, replaced with *https://collaboration.usgs.gov/wg/FCIS/MONKES/default.aspx*). Documentation for the program includes chapters covering the following information: introductory material, a checklist for getting started, downloading the programs, setting up field trips, file management, tip sheets, version history, and system documentation for programmers.

Guidelines for Protecting and Archiving Electronic Data from MONKES programs

As stated above, the use of handheld computers for field data collection improves the overall efficiency of our data collection activities. However, electronic field notes are a significant change in our typical practices, and thus we must remind ourselves of our obligation as federal employees to collect, store, and archive this information for posterity. Procedures must be in place to assure that irreplaceable original data collected in the field are not lost. Instructions for safeguarding files in the field are included in the MONKES1 User Manual, Chapter B 'Setting Paths', for output and backup files. The use of Non-Volatile Memory, such as Compact Flash or Secure Digital data cards, is mandatory for storing data files in the field. Optionally, water-level reports from the MONKES1 program can be printed and stored in site folders.

As with any work flow processes in a Water Science Center, all data handling, backup, and storage procedures should be documented in the Center's Ground-Water Quality Assurance or Data Management Plan, and the Archive Plan. Archiving is defined as the systematic process of storing data to protect it from change or loss. Open File Report 97-11, "A Quality-Assurance Plan for District Ground-Water Activities of the U.S. Geological Survey" outlines the steps to quality assure the archiving process, which includes the establishment and maintenance of a District Archive Plan. Additionally, the process of electronic archiving includes the capability to easily recover the data for future uses. To that end, all XML files produced by MONKES1 are considered to be original data and must be stored online in a directory structure on a Water Science Center server using a standard naming convention. The archive server should be on a regular backup schedule. The following directory structure is provided as an example for the XML archive, where 'party' is the MONKES Party field, and the 'date time' is in the format, YYYYMMDDHHMMSS, for example, 20050302174833.gfeese.OD.xml.

GWARCHIVE

MONKES1 MONKES2 MONKES3

datetime.party.OD.xml datetime.party.OD.xml datetime.party.OD.xml

In addition to the .xml output, MONKES produces a GWSI batch transaction file using the naming convention, datetime.party.gwsi. These files can be recreated at any time from the .xml files, so they need not be archived. A useful tool, a program called MobileSync written by Burl Goree, can be used to make the process of moving files easier. Because many wells often are included within an individual XML file, this file structure will be difficult to search for specific wells. In the future, a script will be written to search on a structure such as this.

In conclusion, the Office of Ground Water recommends the use of MONKES1 for routine ground-water level data collection. Use of the MONKES1 software will improve workflow processes in the collection, processing, and quality assurance of our ground-water data. Systematic backup and archival of the data collected using this software will ensure the reproducibility of these data.

William M. Alley/signed/
Chief, Office of Ground Water

OGW 06.01 Storage of Water-Level Data for Ground Water

February 2, 2006

Office of Water Quality Technical Memorandum No. 2006.01
Office of Ground Water Technical Memorandum No. 2006.01

SUBJECT: Storage of Water-Level Data for Ground Water

This memorandum specifies and clarifies U.S Geological Survey (USGS) requirements for the storage of water-level data collected at wells. The requirements apply to all USGS-related National, regional, and local programs and projects that measure water levels in wells. Projects for which water-level data are collected include studies for which data on water quality, aquifer chemistry, and microbiology might be a primary focus.

STORAGE REQUIREMENTS FOR WATER-LEVEL DATA

All ground-water-level data must be stored in NWIS (Brunett and others, 1997, p. 13), as specified below.

1. All time-series (continuous) ground-water levels that can be stored in the NWIS Automated Data Processing System (ADAPS) must be stored in that database.
    o   ADAPS currently does not accept data collected more frequently than once per second, up to a total of 2881 values per day. Some data sets may exceed this threshold and thus are excluded from this requirement. An example is aquifer-test data. Water levels collected for aquifer tests may be stored outside of NWIS, but must be stored in digital form in the aquifer test archive described in Office of Ground Water Technical Memorandum 94.02.
    o   The tape-down measurement made to calibrate a continuous recorder storing time-series water-level data is to be entered into the NWIS Ground-Water Site Inventory (GWSI).
    o   Beginning with NWIS version 4.5, the discrete water-level data residing in GWSI can be brought into the HYDRA program as a reference data set for quality assuring the continuous water-level data. The policy on editing unit-value data using HYDRA is described in Office of Ground Water Technical Memorandum No. 2005.03.
2. All discrete measurements of ground-water levels collected as part of water-quality as well as ground-water data-collection activities must be stored in GWSI.
    o   Discrete ground-water-level data collected as part of water-quality projects and programs must be entered onto paper or electronic field forms and into GWSI (USGS National Field Manual for the Collection of Water-Quality Data (NFM), Chapters 1.3, 4.2, and 6.0.3). The water-quality field form "Ground-Water Quality Notes" has been modified to provide the

information and codes needed for entry of required data into GWSI. The field form can be accessed at *http://water.usgs.gov/owq/FieldManual/*; under "Announcements." Click on "Water-quality field forms for USGS use."

- o Water-quality personnel also enter their ground-water-level data into QWDATA in order to expedite analysis of their water-quality data within the context of the hydrologic system.
- o Those collecting and managing water-level data are responsible for ensuring that the data entered onto field forms and into the GWSI and QWDATA subsystems of NWIS are correct and consistent.

FUTURE PLANS

The Offices of Ground Water and Water Quality are unified in their goal to avoid duplication of data entry and inconsistency within NWIS subsystems. For example, with version 4.1 of NWIS, water-quality field measurements (pH, dissolved oxygen, etc.) that previously were stored in GWSI were moved electronically into QWDATA. Although a timetable has not been set, the Offices are determined to continue working toward a single-entry system for water-level data.

REFERENCES

Brunett, J.O., Barber, N.L., Burns, A.W, Fogelman, R.P., Gillies, D.C., Lidwin, R.A., and Mack, T.J., 1997, A quality-assurance plan for district ground-water activities of the U.S. Geological Survey: U.S. Geological Survey Open-File Report 97-11, accessed December 14, 2005, at *http://water.usgs.gov/ogw/pubs/OFR9711/*.

Office of Ground Water Technical Memorandum No. 1994.02, Guidance for the preparation, approval, and archiving of aquifer-test results, 1994, accessed December 14, 2005, at *http://water.usgs.gov/admin/memo/GW/gw94.02.html*.

Office of Ground Water Technical Memorandum No. 2005.03, Use of the Program HYDRA to Estimate or Modify Unit Values in ADAPS, 2005, accessed December 14, 2005, at *http://water.usgs.gov/admin/memo/GW/gw05.03.html*.

Wilde, F.D., 2005, Ground Water, Section 1.3 of Chapter 1 (version 1.2, dated 8/2005) in National Field Manual for the Collection of Water-Quality Data, accessed December 14, 2005, at *http://water.usgs.gov/owq/FieldManual/chapter1/Ch1_contents.html*.

Wilde, F.D., Schertz, T.L., and Radtke, D.B., 1999, Quality-Control Samples, Section 4.3 of Chapter 4 (dated 9/1999) in National Field Manual for the Collection of Water-Quality Data, accessed December 14, 2005, at *http://water.usgs.gov/owq/FieldManual/chapter4/html/Ch4_contents.html*.

Wilde, F.D., and Radtke, D.B., 2005, Ground Water, Section 6.0.3 of Chapter 6 (version 1.2, dated 8/2005) in National Field Manual for the Collection of Water-Quality Data, accessed December 14, 2005, at *http://water.usgs.gov/owq/FieldManual/Chapter6/6.0_contents.html*

Timothy L. Miller /s/	William L. Cunningham /s/ for William M. Alley
Chief, Office of Water Quality	Chief, Office of Ground Water

OGW 05.02 PUBLICATIONS--Policy on documenting the results of new simulations using previously

published ground-water models

March 22, 2005

OFFICE OF GROUND WATER TECHNICAL MEMORANDUM NO. 2005.02

Subject: PUBLICATIONS--Policy on documenting the results of new simulations using previously
published ground-water models

The Office of Ground Water has received numerous inquiries about the appropriate level of
documentation required for additional numerical simulations made using a previously published groundwater model (a flow or transport model). The existing policy on documenting the development of a
ground-water model in project reports is stated in Office of Ground Water Technical Memorandum No.
96.04 (*http://water.usgs.gov/admin/memo/GW/gw96.04.html*). However, if a ground-water flow or
transport model has already been developed and documented in a published report to aid in solving a
previous problem, that model may be useful in addressing new questions raised by our cooperators in
managing their resources. The documentation required for additional numerical simulations made using
a previously published ground-water model follows the intent of the original policy but can be
condensed. In this memorandum, "original model" refers to a model that was previously developed and
documented in a published report, and "scenario model" refers to new model simulations using a
previously developed, documented, and published ground-water model. As used here, scenario model
results are based on new stresses, such as the simulation of additional wells, pumping rates, or chemical
sources that differ from the original model. A scenario model does not involve major changes to the
structure of the original model (such as changing the grid, boundary conditions, transmitting properties,
or transport properties used in the model), which would require substantial documentation and
recalibration of the original model.

Scenario model simulations must be documented in a published report to ensure that the simulations are
appropriate for the model, the stresses applied in the simulations are fully described, and the results are
available to the public on an equal basis. Models always involve simplifications and are developed to
answer specific questions. The appropriateness of the model to address new questions must be evaluated
and described in the report. In addition, as stated in Water Resources Division Memorandum No. 94.19,
"Longstanding USGS policy requires that information be released to all interested parties (the public) on
an equal basis, and that no interpretive information be released to the public without prior approval of
the Director." This requirement to publish new findings is reiterated in the U.S. Geological Survey
Manual (*http://www.usgs.gov/usgs-manual/500/500-14.html*) and in Office of Water Information
Technical Memorandum No. 2002.11 on "Reemphasizing the importance of public release of
investigation results"
http://water.usgs.gov/admin/memo/GW/gw05.02.html

In documenting scenario model results, only the aspects of the original model that are changing or are
particularly relevant to the discussion of the adequacy of the model to simulate the new stresses need be
described in the report. A complete re-documentation of the original model construction is not

necessary. The original model can simply be referenced in the scenario model report. All the details of the construction and calibration of the original model need not be reproduced in the new report documenting the scenario model results. The main components of a scenario model report are:

1. A description of the new problem to be evaluated.
2. A justification of the appropriateness of using the original model (with specific attention to the appropriateness of the boundary conditions) to adequately simulate the new problem.
3. A description of the new stresses being simulated and any other changes made to the original model. This description should be complete enough that a reader could independently reproduce the stresses and other changes for the simulation.
4. For transient models, a description of the initial conditions and how they were determined.
5. A description of the simulation results.
6. A discussion of model limitations and the usefulness of the simulation results in answering the problem posed.

In addition, the scenario model must be archived in accordance with Office of Ground Water Technical Memorandum No. 00.02 on the archiving of models (*http://water.usgs.gov/admin/memo/GW/gw00.02.html*).

In many cases, reports documenting scenario models can be relatively short and concise, and can be released online-only, if desired. These reports, whether online-only or printed, must address the critical elements listed above, and they must go through the complete USGS report review and approval process.

William M. Alley /s/
Chief, Office of Ground Water

OGW 03.03 Agreement Forms for Gaging Station and Observation Well Installations and Transfers

Agreement Forms for Gaging Station and Observation Well Installations and Transfers

September 17, 2003

Office of Surface Water Technical Memorandum No. 2003.08
Office of Ground Water Technical Memorandum No. 2003.03

Subject: Agreement Forms for Gaging Station and Observation Well Installations and Transfers

The purpose of this memorandum is to announce the availability of updated agreement forms that should be used for installation of and transfer of ownership of WRD gaging stations or observation wells. These forms, identified below, retain their previously assigned U.S. Geological Survey Form Numbers and must be accessed through the USGS forms page, *https://gsvaresa01.er.usgs.gov/Welcome.nsf?Open.*

The updated forms correct weaknesses identified in the lawsuit "Laurence v. USA et al", which involved a personal injury at a (former) USGS gaging station that had been transferred to the Placer County Water Agency (California). They also reflect the Solicitor's recommendation to use simpler, more direct language. The underlying established WRD policies on property use and transfer agreements remain unchanged until such time as they are superseded by new Bureau policy.

1. U.S. Geological Survey Form Number: 9-1482
   Title: Agreement for Installation and Maintenance of Gaging Station

   · Reference: *wrdpolicy94.008.html*, dated Feb. 18, 1994
   · Approval authority: District Chief
   · **Note:** For the purpose of this agreement, "gaging station" includes
   all stilling wells and structures, including cableways and equipment, used in
   the operation and maintenance of the monitoring site.

2. U.S. Geological Survey Form Number: 9-1483
   Title: Well Drilling/Sampling Agreement

   · Reference: wrdpolicy94.008.html, dated Feb. 18, 1994
   · Approval authority: District Chief
   · **Note:** During the first 5 years of the agreement only the government
   may terminate, after 5 years both parties may terminate.

3. U.S. Geological Survey Form Number: 9-3106
   Title: Well Transfer Agreement

   · Reference: wrdpolicy87.017.html, dated Jan. 15, 1987
   · Approval authority: Regional Hydrologist
   · **Notes:**

a. Well transfers to private parties are not authorized during the first 5 years of the agreement.

b. USGS employees are not authorized to give away government property. All equipment not part of the well structure (for example, recorders and sensing devices) should be retained by USGS and not transferred with the well.

4. U.S. Geological Survey Form Numbers:

9-3107   Title: Gage Transfer Agreement
9-3107-a   Title: Gage Transfer Agreement to a Federal Agency

· Reference: wrdpolicy92.012.html, dated Dec. 06, 1991
· Approval authority: Regional Hydrologist
· Notes:

a. The Gaging Station transfer requires the USGS to share pertinent safety policies and procedures with the transferee, and requires the transferee to perform his own independent engineering analysis regarding the identification of design or structural deficiencies, and the suitability of the gaging station for the use intended. A memorandum to the record is recommended stating: (1) why the gaging station was transferred; (2) that no equipment was transferred with the gaging station; (3) that [a list of] safety policies and guidelines pertaining to the gaging station were provided to the Transferee; and (4) the date that permission for the transfer was obtained from the Region. A copy of the signed transfer agreement and the Transferee's landowner permission agreement shall be filed with this memorandum.

b. The form 9-3107 should be used to transfer a gaging station to state, local, or tribal government agency or Federal Energy Regulatory Commission licensee. Form 9-3107a should be used to transfer a gage to another Federal agency.

c. USGS employees are not authorized to give away government property. All equipment owned by the USGS that is not part of the gaging station structure (for example, recorders and sensing devices) should be retained by USGS and not transferred with the gaging station.

d. The Transferee, if not the landowner, must obtain written permission from the landowner to operate and maintain the gaging station.

/signed by Robert R. Mason/   /signed by William L. Cunningham/

Stephen F. Blanchard   William M. Alley
Chief, Office of Surface Water   Chief, Office of Ground Water

PROGRAMS AND PLANS-Establishment of a National Policy to Archive Borehole-Geophysical Logs

September 27, 2000

OFFICE OF GROUND WATER TECHNICAL MEMORANDUM 00.03

Subject: PROGRAMS AND PLANS-Establishment of a National Policy to Archive
 Borehole-Geophysical Logs

Borehole-geophysical logging is an important part of many geologic and hydrologic investigations. Increasingly, geophysical logs are collected as digital data rather than paper analog charts. At present, the U.S. Geological Survey (USGS) has no standardized format for storing digital geophysical logs. Establishment of a standard format for storing digital logs is important for the future development and application of USGS geophysical databases. This memorandum presents such standards and establishes the policy that all digital geophysical logs collected after October 30, 2000 be archived in a District database following these standards. The standard format has been designed to include the necessary information, to correspond to but not duplicate what is stored in the National Water Information System (NWIS), and to be flexible so as to not greatly increase manual data entry.

The borehole-geophysical log archive must be in ASCII format and consist of the following:

1. Header that includes the NWIS site ID, station name, and other ID; logging operation and procedures; log-measuring point; magnetic declination; borehole and hydrologic conditions at the time of logging; and probe and calibration/standardization information (probe type and serial number and calibration/standardization date, standard, and response).
2. Data-identification heading that immediately precedes the data records and describes the data by column and includes a depth column heading followed by log parameter column heading(s); the column headings consist of two lines, parameter names on the top and corresponding units below.
3. Data records that include depth values and corresponding data values for one or more log parameters.

ASCII headings and data records generated following the Log ASCII Standard (*http://www.cwls.org/las-info.html*) and other common digital logging formats are acceptable for archiving purposes. An example log archive entry is shown in Attachment A.

An NWIS site must be established for the logged borehole. Borehole construction greatly affects geophysical log response. Many boreholes are logged prior to their final completion so timing and details of construction in relation to log-data collection is critical for log analysis. The casing and opening type, depth, and diameter data for the hole at the time of logging must be part of the construction data sequence entries in NWIS. Information on logging operation and procedures, log-measuring point, magnetic declination for magnetically oriented logs, borehole and hydrologic conditions, and probe calibration/standardization also is critical for log analysis but presently is not stored in NWIS. This information, therefore, must be stored as part of the log header.

As shown in the example (Attachment A), any pre-existing log headers should be included after the standard header and before the headings and data records. In most cases, digital logs can be easily entered into the data archive by simply adding the standard header in front of the log-data file. A log header entry program has been developed to aid in the generation of the standard header.

Some digital log data such as acoustic- and optical-televiewer and borehole-radar data are not conducive for conversion to a standard format, so they will need to be archived in their existing form. Software needed to display and analyze such log data should be identified in the log header.

Each District will set up an archive on a locally based computer system. The archive will consist of a main directory called LOGARCHIVE. Each geophysical log file name will include the NWIS 15-digit Site ID number, date of log collection (year month day), two-letter log-type code, and sequence number extension. The first log of the same type collected on a particular day would have a sequence number of 01, the second, 02, etc. The path name for the example entry shown in Attachment A would be:

LOGARCHIVE>424531077564201.20000601.MI01

An executable file of any software needed for analysis of non-standard log files should be included in the LOGARCHIVE with explanation of security measures for proprietary programs.

The log header entry program may be downloaded from the Office of Ground Water (OGW) internal web page (*http://water.usgs.gov/usgs/ogw*). The master lists of geophysical log-type codes and heading-log parameters and units also will be maintained on the OGW web page. Requests for additional log types and parameters should be directed to the OGW Borehole Geophysics Advisor (*jhwillia@usgs.gov*). The Regional Ground-Water Specialists are to act on behalf of the Office of Ground Water to assure that the borehole-geophysical logs collected by the Districts are properly archived.

Adherence to the policy of archiving borehole-geophysical logs will ensure that data collected by District offices will remain available for support of published reports, future scientific investigations, and data requests from the public.

William M. Alley
Chief, Office of Ground Water

Attachment

Distribution: A (without attachment)
DC, Regional Ground-Water Specialists, NR, SR, CR, WR
Chief, Branch of Geophysical Applications and Support, CT
John Williams, NY

Attachment A   Example log archive

U.S. GEOLOGICAL SURVEY
GEOPHYSICAL LOG
(output from log header entry program)

Site ID (C1): 424531077564201
Station name (C12): 515
Other ID (C190): MW-8
Date of log: 06-01-00
Start time of log: 15:35
Office/logging unit: USGS Any District
Logging operator: Jane Smith
Observer: John Doe

Description of log-measuring point: Land Surface
Height of log-measuring point above/below land-surface datum: 0.0 FT
Altitude of log-measuring point (NGVD): 516.0 FT
Log orientation: Magnetic North
Magnetic declination: 10
Logging direction: UP
Logging speed: 20 FT/MIN
Depth error after logging: 0.8 FT

Logging probe manufacturer: Century
Logging probe model: EM Induction, Gamma #9510
Logging probe serial number: 746
Description of calibration/standardization: Century Calibration Ring
Date of calibration/standardization: 06-01-2000
Standard: 0 ms/M
Response: 72775 CPS
Standard: 690 ms/M
Response: 110400 CPS

Borehole fluid type: WATER
Depth of borehole fluid below log-measuring point: 364 FT
Borehole fluid resistivity/conductivity: 8 OHM-M
Borehole fluid temperature: 53.5 F
Hydrologic conditions: Mine-room roof collapse resulted in flooding of the
mine and major drawdown
in the overlying aquifers.
Software for non-ASCII logs: NA
Remarks: Borehole is 200 ft southwest of the edge of the sinkhole formed by
the mine-roof collapse.

Attachment A (cont.)
(pre-existing log header--from logging software)

```
COMPANY      : US GEOLOGICAL SURVEY
WELL      : MW-8
LOCATION/FIELD : SALTVILLE
COUNTY      : SALT
STATE      : ANY
SECTION      :      TOWNSHIP      :      RANGE :
DATE      : 06/01/00   ELEV. PERM. DATUM :
DEPTH DRILLER : 702      LOG MEASURED FROM: LSD  GL
LOG BOTTOM    : 701.9    DRL MEASURED FROM:
LOG TOP      : 516.7    LOGGING UNIT   : ANY    TYPE : 9510C
CASING DRILLER : 520      FIELD OFFICE    : ANY    THRESH:
CASING TYPE   : STEEL     RECORDED BY     : JANE SMITH
CASING THICKNESS :      BOREHOLE FLUID   : WATER
BIT SIZE      : 6
```

```
DEPTH      GAM(NAT) COND    RES(FL)
```
Data identification heading
```
  FT      CPS      MMHO/M  OHM-M

  516.7   21       5552.334 0.180
  516.8   40       5543.827 0.180
```
. . . .
ASCII data
. . . .
```
  701.8   210      27.428   36.459
  701.9   245      28.732   34.804
```

PROGRAMS AND PLANS--Update of the National Policy to Archive Ground Water Flow and
Transport Models

OFFICE OF GROUND WATER TECHNICAL MEMORANDUM NO. 00.02

Subject: PROGRAMS AND PLANS--Update of the National Policy to Archive Ground Water Flow
and Transport Models

INTRODUCTION

Office of Ground Water Technical Memorandum 93.01 established a policy for archiving ground-water
flow and transport models. Although the fundamental policy remains the same, there is a need to update
the policy to account for changes in storage technology and the wider use of supporting software to
generate input data for the models. Rather than describing only the changes, this memorandum contains
the complete revised policy.

POLICY

Ground-water flow and transport models are an integral part of our interpretive ground-water
investigations, and the results of these models form the basis for many of the conclusions published in
U.S. Geological Survey reports. The numerical data and related information that comprise these models
need to remain available to: (1) support and validate the results in published reports, (2) assure that
working versions of all models are available for future scientific use, and (3) assure that the data are
available to the public when requested. The appropriate model data and related information are to be
stored in a permanent, well-documented manner to ensure their continued availability.

All ground-water flow and transport models that are a significant part of ground-water investigations
with completion dates of October 1993 or later are to be included in a model archive. The Regional
Ground Water Specialists are to act on behalf of the Office of Ground Water to assure that all required
information is present in the archive. Status of the archives also will be examined as a routine part of
District ground-water discipline reviews. Implementation requirements for the archive are presented in
an Attachment to this memorandum.

The archive is for internal Water Resources Division (WRD) access and use. The release of information
from the archive is subject to compliance with any existing WRD policies that may apply to the public
release of such information. For example, the archive can be used to provide the public with input data
for model simulations that are described in a published report. Other data in the archive that were not
directly used as model input may require additional documentation prior to release. For example,
geographic information system (GIS) data that were used to create model input files may be stored in
the archive, but such data could contain interpretive information that was not documented in the model
report.

The ground-water model archive does not relieve individual investigators of the need to fully describe and document model analyses in their reports.

William M. Alley
Chief, Office of Ground Water

Attachment

WRD Distribution: A, B, S, FO, PO
Regional Ground Water Specialists, NR, CR, SR, WR

This memorandum supersedes Office of Ground Water Technical Memorandum No. 93.01

ATTACHMENT

IMPLEMENTATION OF DISTRICT GROUND WATER MODEL ARCHIVES

Each District will set up an on-line archive on a locally based computer. The archive must be located on disks that are routinely backed up as done for other mission critical information. Optical disk storage cannot be used as a substitute for on-line storage.

The archive will consist of a main directory. The suggested name for this is GWMARCHIVE; however, another name can be used if desired. A report subdirectory, located directly below the main directory, will be established for each published report containing a ground-water flow or transport model analysis. Each report subdirectory should be given a name that clearly reflects the U.S. Geological Survey report number.

A subdirectory named CONTENTS, located immediately below each report directory, will include one or more files that contain: (1) the full reference for the subject report; (2) descriptions of the subdirectory structure and of the files contained in each subdirectory, (3) descriptions of data file formats, when appropriate; (4) the sequence of model runs; and (5) instructions for running simulations.

The archive must include the model source codes, input files, macros and operating files such as UNIX shell codes and personal computer batch (BAT) files, and model output files for each simulation described in the report. These simulations will include (when applicable) the final calibrated steady-state and transient results and any predictive results described in the publication. Model results of minor importance, such as interim calibration runs, should not be archived. The model output files are included to allow future verification that the model reproduces the published results when the input files are rerun. Input files must be stored as read by the model. Typically the input files will use an ASCII format. In cases where model input files are proprietary or machine-dependent, ASCII versions of the files should also be stored in the archive if it is possible to generate them. The ASCII version will make it more likely that the files can be used on virtually any computer without the need for specialized or proprietary software.

The storage of additional ancillary data is optional, but is strongly encouraged. Examples of ancillary data that might be stored are GIS data files, data stored by pre-processor codes, or other data directly related to the model simulations. Where possible, these data should be stored in a widely supported format as opposed to a proprietary format. For example ARC/INFO offers the ability to export GIS data stored in their proprietary coverage format into formats that can be read by other applications. If ancillary data are stored elsewhere in permanent USGS storage systems, then there is no need to duplicate the storage in the model archive. Documentation of ancillary data must include a description, the source, format, the version of software on which it was produced, etc.

When the input data of one model depends directly on output from another model, both models are to be included in the archive. If the models are documented in separate reports, a cross-reference between the reports must be included in the CONTENTS directory of the archive entry for each report.

The appropriate model files must reside in the District archive when the report is submitted to the Region for approval. If additional model simulations are required as a contingency for approval, these simulations should replace, or be added to the archive as appropriate.

OFFICE OF GROUND WATER TECHNICAL MEMORANDUM NO. 98.02

SUBJECT: Data Elements for Ground-Water Sites

This memorandum describes Mandatory and Recommended data elements
for ground-water sites in the Ground-Water Site Inventory (GWSI)
for the purpose of standardizing the informational content of
GWSI. Entry of mandatory and recommended data elements into GWSI
as described in this memorandum applies as of the date of this
memorandum. However, data elements designated as 'Planned' are
scheduled for future releases of the National Water Information
System (NWIS) and would be entered once these data elements can
be populated in GWSI.

Background

Three categories of data are populated with ground-water site
information in GWSI. The first category consists of mandatory
data elements. Mandatory data elements are those that must be
populated to establish a site in NWIS and to enable entry of
other data into the system. The second category consists of
recommended data elements. The minimum recommended data elements
are those data elements in GWSI that provide additional basic
information about a ground-water site. Input of these elements
is strongly recommended. The third category consists of other
data elements, which are all of the remaining data fields
available in GWSI. These data enhance the basic information
about the site and are populated in GWSI to the extent available.

Mandatory and Recommended Categories

Mandatory data elements: Sixteen data elements for a ground-water
site must be populated to establish a site in NWIS and to enable
entry of other data into the system (table 1).

Table 1. Mandatory ground-water data elements

[GWSI, Ground-Water Site Inventory; HUC, Hydrologic Unit Code;
GMT, Greenwich Mean Time; GIS, Geographic Information System; The
component number in GWSI associated with each data element is
included for reference (Mathey, 1989)]

Mandatory data element (Component)	Comment number in GWSI)
Source agency code (C4)	
Site identification (C1)	
Station name (C12)	
Latitude (C9)	
Longitude (C10)	
Latitude and longitude accuracy (C11)	
Horizontal datum (C36)	Scheduled for NWIS release 3_1.
Method of determining horizontal datum (C35)	Scheduled for NWIS release 3_1.
State (C7)	
County (C8)	
HUC (C20)	Not mandatory until link to GIS becomes available.
Station type (C802)	
GMT offset (C813)	
Data reliability (C3)	
Site type (C2)	
Use of site (C23)	

Recommended data elements: Fifteen data elements for a ground-water site are strongly recommended for entry into GWSI (table 2). Some recommended data elements, if populated, also must include a subset of mandatory data elements associated with that recommended data element. The recommended data elements are those that provide additional basic information about a ground-water site: for example, owner of the well, information about the installation and construction of the well, information about subsurface geohydrologic units at the site, and water levels.

Table 2. Recommended ground-water data elements and related mandatory and recommended subsets.

[GWSI, ground-water site inventory; The component number in GWSI associated with each data element is included for reference (Mathey, 1989)]

Recommended data element (Component number in GWSI)	Mandatory subset (Component number in GWSI)	Recommended subset (Component number in GWSI)
SITE FILE		
Project code (C5)		
Altitude of site (C16)	Date altitude determined (Planned)*2 Altitude method (C17) Altitude accuracy (C18) Source of altitude (Planned)*2 Altitude datum (C22)*1	
Date of inventory (C711)		
Use of water (C24)		
Hole depth (C27)		
Depth of well (C28)	Date measured or reported for any new record (Planned) *2	Measurement accuracy (Planned) *2 Source of depth data (C29)
CONSTRUCTION		
Construction data		Completion date (year/month) (C60) Method of construction (C65) Source of data (C64)

Hole data	Depth to the top of hole interval (C73)	Depth to bottom of hole interval (C74)
		Hole diameter (C75)
		Source of data (Planned) *2
Casing data	Top of casing (C77)	Diameter (C79)
		Casing material (C80)
		Source of data (Planned) *2
Openings data	Depth to top of interval (C83)	Depth to bottom of interval (C84)
	Type of opening (C85)	Source of data (Planned) *2

MISCELLANEOUS

| Owner data | Owner name (C161) | Date of ownership (C159) |
| Logs data (includes geologic and geophysical logs) | Type of log (C199) | Flag that log exists in a separate data base, with links to that record (Planned) *2 |

DISCHARGE

Discharge data	Discharge (C150)	Measurement accuracy (Planned) *2
	Measurement method (C152)	Source of data (C151)
	Date discharge measured (C148)	
	Type of discharge (C703)	

GEOHYDROLOGY

| Geohydrologic unit Data | Unit identifier or name (C93) | Contributing unit (C304) |
| | | Source of data (Planned) *2 |

WATER LEVELS

Water-level data

Water level (C237)
Measurement method (C239)
Water-level accuracy (C276)
Year of measurement (C235)
Source of water-level measurement (C244) *1
Altitude of site (C16)
Date altitude determined (Planned) *2
Altitude method (C17)
Altitude accuracy (C18)
Source of altitude (Planned) *2
Altitude datum (C22) *1

Site status (C238)
Agency (Planned) *2
Month and day measured (C235)
Time of measurement (C709)

---

*1 Scheduled for NWIS release 3_1.
*2 Scheduled for a future NWIS release.

Reference Cited

Mathey, S.B. (editor), 1989, National Water Information System Users Manual, Volume 2, Chapter 4, Ground-Water Site Inventory System: U.S. Geological Survey Open-File Report 89-587, 227 p.

/s/ K.J. Hollett for
William M. Alley
Chief, Office of Ground Water

OGW 94.02 Guidance for the preparation, approval, and archiving of aquifer-test results

June 2, 1994

OFFICE OF GROUND WATER TECHNICAL MEMORANDUM 94.02

Subject: Guidance for the preparation, approval, and archiving of aquifer-test results

Analyses of aquifer tests to define the hydraulic characteristics of a specific aquifer or aquifer system are an integral part of our interpretive ground-water investigations. The results of these analyses are critical components of flow-system or solute-transport analyses and important to conclusions published in U.S. Geological Survey (USGS) reports. Consequently, reported aquifer characteristics such as hydraulic conductivity, transmissivity, storativity and other hydraulic characteristics derived from aquifer-test analyses must be clearly documented and technically defensible. The purpose of this memorandum is to describe guidelines and procedures necessary to obtain approval for the results of aquifer tests analyzed by employees of the Water Resources Division (WRD) and to provide guidelines for archival of the test results.

BACKGROUND

According to WRD Publications Guide (Article 11.01.2) "....calculated hydraulic characteristics such as transmissivity, hydraulic conductivity, and storage coefficient, are interpretive and must be approved by the Director, unless cited from a Director-approved report." In a memorandum dated March 11, 1992, the Assistant Chief Hydrologist, Scientific Information Management, delegated authority to approve aquifer-test results to the Regional Hydrologists. Approval is required for all calculations of aquifer-hydraulic characteristics to be released to the general public, to cooperators, or published in or otherwise used to support the results of investigations reported in USGS-approved reports.

Estimates of aquifer-hydraulic characteristics commonly are obtained from "textbook" or published values for various lithologies. These are not considered calculations of aquifer characteristics and do not require approval under the terms of this memorandum. In addition, estimates of transmissivity determined on the basis of specific-capacity measurements do not require approval.

DOCUMENTATION, APPROVAL, AND ARCHIVAL OF AQUIFER-TEST RESULTS

While the USGS encourages the publication of aquifer-test results, it is not feasible to publish the data and graphical results for every test conducted. In all cases, either as part of a formal report or as a separate packet, aquifer-test results should be submitted to the Regional Ground-Water Specialist for review and subsequent approval by the Regional Hydrologist. The Regional Ground-Water Specialist reviews the report manuscript or aquifer-test packet to assess (1) that the report or packet contains the necessary data and related information to properly analyze the subject test(s), and (2) that the analyses and results are technically defensible.

Elements that typically should be submitted for review are listed below. These elements assume an aquifer test comprising a pumping well and one or more observation wells and should be modified as appropriate for other types of tests such as a single-well slug test. The eight elements are as follows.

1. A brief description of the test (this can be neatly hand written) which includes the purpose, date, test procedures, and methods of analysis of the results. Any unique or unusual features or problems related to the test or to the collection and analysis of test data should be described. A brief description of the assumptions used in analyzing the test results also should be included, as needed to clarify the test.

2. A sketch of the test site showing the distances from the pumped well to all observation wells and the location of any boundaries, streams, springs, ditches, pumping or flowing wells, or other features that possibly could influence test results. Where the test includes multiple wells, the sketch of the test site should be drawn to scale.

3. Description of test and observation well construction, including screened and open interval(s), casing and screen diameters, and location of filter pack and grouted intervals.

4. A description of the site hydrogeologic characteristics, including sections that show the major water-bearing and confining zones or units. The intervals of the pumping and observation wells that are screened or open should be depicted on the logs or sections.

5. Time-discharge records of the pumped well (all measurements, not just average discharge).

6. Water-level records and hydrographs showing pre-test trends and water levels during the pumping and recovery phases.

7. Description of methods and computations showing adjustments to drawdown for pre-test trends, adjustments of recovery for projected drawdown, or adjustments to account for extraneous effects not related to pumping or recovery, such as barometric and tidal effects or other interferences.

8. All plots of observed or adjusted drawdown or recovery data used to determine hydraulic characteristics, showing match points, when used, and computations.

It is recognized that in some cases it is not possible to provide a complete description of these eight elements. Investigators are encouraged to discuss their plans with the Regional Ground-Water Specialist to determine the requirements for a particular test packet or report before they forward it for review and approval.

A transmittal memorandum, indicating that the test results have been reviewed by the District or Area ground-water specialist or his or her designee, should be included with the test packet or report. This review should include at least some checking of the field data and a verification that the test results are appropriate, given the site hydrogeology, well construction, and test conditions and that the test results have been reviewed independently before being submitted for regional review and approval.

Following approval by the Regional Hydrologist, the packet or report will be returned to the originating District or Office where the hydraulic characteristics and related site and well data should be entered into the Ground-Water Site Inventory System or National Water Information System (NWIS) and the packet and associated information appropriately archived in a District "aquifer-test file." These archived aquifer-test files should include the draft-report routing sheet or packet-review transmittal memorandum. Districts also are encouraged to archive test analyses and results completed prior to this memorandum. The aquifer-test files will be reviewed as a routine part of District ground-water discipline reviews.

If computer software is used in the aquifer-test analysis, the policy outlined in Office of Ground Water Technical Memorandum 91.04, dated August 14, 1991, must be followed. This policy requires that the theoretical basis of the software be documented and that it be demonstrated that a test-data set can be correctly analyzed using the software. Submittal of a computer-software analysis does not eliminate the need for the information described in item element 8, above.

This memorandum discusses information needs in the context of single- or multiple-well aquifer tests. Aquifer characteristics also may be calculated by other methods, such as, determination of aquifer diffusivity from attenuation of a tidal pulse or flood wave through an aquifer, or using hydrograph-recession characteristics. The same review procedures should be followed for these types of analyses, and information in the report manuscript or packet must be adequate to enable reviewers to visualize the physical system, evaluate all data, verify all calculations, and assess that the methods and results are defensible.

Sincerely,

William M. Alley
Chief, Office of
Ground Water

OGW 93.03 Interim Policy Memorandum about Storing Data in the National Water Information System

January 25, 1993

OFFICE OF GROUND WATER TECHNICAL MEMORANDUM NO. 93.03

Subject: Interim Policy Memorandum about Storing Data in the National Water Information System

The purpose of this memorandum is to restate and clarify existing policy regarding the use of the National Water Information System (NWIS) to store ground-water data collected by the U.S. Geological Survey, Water Resources Division (WRD).

Problems and Concerns

Discipline reviews are finding that not all ground-water data collected by WRD are being stored in NWIS. It appears that some elements of policy detailed in WRD Memorandum Nos. 76.44, 77.136, 83.89, and 86.28 have been misunderstood and have not been vigorously enforced at the Regional and Headquarters levels.

Clarification and Restatement of Policy

WRD Memorandum 92.59 has recently been released and states that the recommendations made by the Data Policy Committee (Open-File Report 92-56) have been accepted as official policy. That policy includes the following:

   "The current policy in WRD is that all water data collected as part of the routine data collection of the WRD (both basic and project data) must be stored in the computer files of the National Water Information System. One purpose of this policy is to enable all WRD work to be verifiable and repeatable to the greatest extent possible at any time in the future."

The Office of Ground Water (OGW) interprets routine data collection of the WRDS to include all ground-water data collected by WRD basic data programs and District projects. Any request for exemption from this policy must be approved by OGW. The only exceptions to this requirement are proprietary data, and data that cannot be stored in NWIS because they do not functionally fit. When the new version II of NWIS software is completed, it is expected that many of the ground-water data that WRD collects will functionally fit in NWIS, including many types of geophysical, hydrogeological, and hydraulic test data.

Implementation of Policy

The OGW and the Regional Ground-Water Specialists will review compliance with this policy during District technical and selected project reviews and by actual interrogation of NWIS. Several recent District reviews by OGW have included an additional person on the review team for the purpose of examining data-related issues. The OGW has added a staff person to specifically address the issues of data and data bases. The OGW also has created the Ground-Water Data Committee to develop recommendations about issues of policy and management of ground-water data. Future memorandums will address other aspects of ground-water data policy.

William M. Alley
Acting Chief, Office
of Ground Water

October 28, 1992

OFFICE OF GROUND WATER TECHNICAL MEMORANDUM NO. 93.01

Subject: PROGRAMS AND PLANS--Establishment of a National Policy to Archive Ground-Water Flow and Transport Models

POLICY

Ground-water flow and transport models are an integral part of our interpretive ground-water investigations, and the results of these models form the basis for many of the conclusions published in U.S. Geological Survey reports. The numerical data and related information that comprise these models need to remain available to: (1) support and validate the results in published reports, (2) assure that working versions of all models are available for future scientific use, and (3) assure that the data are available to the public when requested. The appropriate model data and related information are to be stored in a permanent, well- documented manner to ensure their continued availability.

Effective as of the date of this memorandum, a national ground- water model archive is established. All ground-water flow and transport models that are a significant part of ground-water investigations with completion dates of October 1993 or later are to be included in the archive. Where feasible, districts also should archive models from completed investigations and from current projects to be completed prior to October 1993. The Regional Ground Water Specialists are to act on behalf of the Office of Ground Water to assure that all required information is present in the archive. Status of the archives also will be examined as a routine part of district ground-water discipline reviews. Design and implementation requirements for the archive are presented in Attachments 1 and 2 to this memorandum.

The archive is for internal Water Resources Division (WRD) access and use and is to serve as the source of ground-water model data supplied to the public upon request. The public release of specific information contained in the archive is subject to compliance with any existing WRD policies that may apply to the public release of such information.

The ground-water model archive does not relieve individual investigators of the need to fully describe and document model analyses in their reports.

Joseph S. Rosenshein
Acting Chief, Office
of Ground Water
2 Attachments

WRD Distribution: A, B, S, FO, PO

ATTACHMENT 1

DESIGN AND IMPLEMENTATION OF DISTRICT GROUND WATER MODEL ARCHIVES

STRUCTURE AND CONTENTS:

The archive will consist of a main directory called GWMARCIV. A report subdirectory, located directly below GWMARCIV, will be established for each published report containing a ground-water flow or transport model analysis. Each report subdirectory should be given a name that clearly reflects the U.S. Geological Survey report number. The archive must include the model source codes, input files, macros and operating files such as JCL, CPL, and UNIX shell codes, and model output files for each simulation described in the report. These simulations will include (when applicable) the final calibrated steady-state and transient results and any predictive results described in the publication. Model results of minor importance, such as interim calibration runs, should not be archived. Model output will be archived for future verification that the input data files properly reproduce the published results when the input files are rerun. The storage of additional ancillary data is optional, but is strongly encouraged. Examples of ancillary data that might be stored are pertinent pre- and post-processor codes, related data, or other files directly related to the model simulations.

A subdirectory named CONTENTS, located immediately below each report directory, will include one or more files that contain:

(1) the full reference for the subject report; (2) descriptions of the subdirectory structure and of the files contained in each subdirectory, (3) descriptions of data file formats, when appropriate; (4) the sequence of model runs; and (5) instructions for running simulations. Attachment 2 shows one example of what an archive directory structure might look like for a typical project.

When the input data of one model depends directly on output from another model, both models are to be included in the archive. If the models are documented in separate reports, a cross-reference between the reports must be included in the CONTENTS directory of the archive entry for each report.

Model input files must be stored in ASCII format to assure that they can be processed in the future on virtually any computer without the need for specialized or proprietary software. In cases where model input files are derived from either proprietary or machine-dependent software, ASCII versions of the model input files must be included in the archive.

IMPLEMENTATION:

Each district will set up an archive on a locally based computer. The district staff is responsible for designing a subdirectory structure that permits efficient and logical storage of the required information for each specific model. Files will be accumulated and stored in the on-line archive until the final interpretive report is approved, after which time the files are to be moved to permanent storage.

For all studies with completion dates of October 1993 or later, the appropriate model files must reside on-line in the district archive when the report is submitted to the Region for approval. Verification of compliance with this policy is the responsibility of the Regional Ground Water Specialists. Reports returned to the district for revision that require new or additional model simulations will require an archive update.

Upon final approval of the interpretive report, the archive is to be copied to permanent storage on an optical disk using WORM (write once, read many) technology. A copy of the WORM disk will remain in the originating district to service requests for data, and a duplicate copy will be furnished to the Region for off-site backup. A WORM disk may contain model data for one or more published reports provided the disk is indexed appropriately. The archive may be transferred to tape as a short-term storage option if the district does not have immediate access to WORM disk production equipment. The period of interim storage on tape should not exceed 1 year. The archive process is considered complete only when a WORM disk has been produced. On-line storage of the archived data may be discontinued at the discretion of the district following transfer of the archive to WORM disk or to interim tape storage.

OGW 92.06 General Policy for the Use of the Ground Water Site Inventory System

March 19, 1992

OFFICE OF GROUND WATER TECHNICAL MEMORANDUM 92.06

Subject: General Policy for the Use of the Ground Water Site Inventory System

The purpose of this technical memorandum is to establish an overall policy for the use of the Ground Water Site Inventory (GWSI) of the National Water Information System I (NWIS-I) for operational activities of the Water Resources Division. This policy will have application as well to the GWSI in NWIS-II when it becomes operational.

The need for quality-assured data from all of the Division's water-resources activities is critical for addressing the Nation's water problems. Recently, the States were given the responsibility from the U.S. Environmental Protection Agency to develop their individual ground-water protection and management strategies. The technical development of these strategies will depend heavily on data and information from the Geological Survey. This effort will be ongoing during the period that the Division will be making the transition from the NWIS-I to the NWIS-II data bases.

A recent report, "Review of the U.S. Geological Survey's Ground-Water Site Inventory Data Base," by Robert Faye and Keith McFadden indicated that the GWSI data base is irregularly populated among the districts, large differences exist between the GWIS in NWIS and National Water Data Storage and Retrieval System (WATSTORE) data bases, and few districts have a well-defined policy on the population and use of the ground-water data bases.

To begin to address the irregular population of GWSI, from this date forward ground-water data from all active projects shall use GWSI for data storage and retrieval. Site data for all wells in water-level observation networks must be entered in GWSI. In addition, continuous records for all observation wells must be entered in the daily values files of NWIS. Site information for individual wells and springs for which data are to be shown in published reports must be entered into GWSI.

Additional Office of Ground Water technical memorandums will be issued that address specific procedures for the collection of ground-water data in the field, checking and verification of field data, entry of ground-water data into the GWSI, checking and verification of data entry, entry of past paper file data, and other aspects of ground-water data collection and storage as needed.

/s/ Joseph S. Rosenshein
Acting Chief, Office of
Ground Water

Appendix 3. Groundwater Tool Box; Recommended Contents

The WAWSC maintains several sets of groundwater field equipment. An example of the equipment contained in a set is listed below (list from Drost, 2005):

Measuring Equipment:

- Steel measuring tapes; 100, 300, and 500 ft (if needed)
- Electric sounding tape; Waterline 300 ft, Waterline 1,000 ft (if needed)
- Pocket measuring tape (engineering scale)
- Air tank (and tie-downs)
- Pressure gage and regulator
- Bicycle pump
- Rags
- Carpenter's chalk
- Measuring tape weights and spares (sausage-style; brass, copper, or stainless steel)
- Sounding weight and attaching wire
- Field instruction manual
- Paintstick (for marking measuring point)

Disinfecting equipment:

- Bleach container, 5 gal
- Household bleach
- Tech and Chem-wipes
- Latex gloves

Safety Equipment:

- Visual identity clothing (hat, vest, jacket, and/or shirt)
- Safety glasses
- Hantavirus kit:
- Half-mask respirators (small and large) and replacement filters
- Latex gloves
- Protective goggles
- Alcohol wipes
- Spray bottle for bleach solution

Office Supplies:

- Calculator
- Clipboard
- Pencils, pens, etc.
- Well-location map overlay and scale

Miscellaneous Equipment:

- GPS unit

- Plastic garbage bags
- Paper towels
- Raincoat (x-large)
- Bucket, 5-gal, plastic
- Hand cleaner

Tools:

- WD-40
- Set of screwdrivers
- Gloves
- Well plugs (assorted sizes)
- Bolts and nuts (assorted sizes)
- Set of Allen wrenches (standard)
- Set of Allen wrenches (metric)
- Socket wrenches (standard)
- Socket wrenches (metric)
- Machete
- Pipe wrenches (8-, 10-, 14-, 18-, and 24-in.)
- Crescent wrenches (6-, 8-, 10-, and 12-in.)
- Crow bar
- Batteries (spares for GPS [4 AA], flashlight [2 C], and e-tape [1 9V])
- File
- Shovel
- Pry bar
- Hack saw
- Whiskbroom
- Duct tape
- Electrical tape
- Flashlight
- Wire brush
- Hammer
- Pliers
- Chisel
- Miscellaneous additional tools